DECORATIVE PAINTING *for the Home*

DECORATIVE PAINTING
for the Home

Creating Exciting Effects with
Water-Based Paints

Lee Andre &
David Lipe

Sterling Publishing Co., Inc.   New York
A STERLING/LARK BOOK

Editor: Leslie Dierks
Art Director: Chris Colando
Photography: Mark Eifert
Illustrations: Chris Colando
Production: Chris Colando

Library of Congress Cataloging-in-Publication Data
Andre, Lee, 1966–
    Decorative painting for the home : creating exciting effects with
water-based paints / Lee Andre & David Lipe.
      p.   cm.
    "A Sterling/Lark book."
    Includes index.
    ISBN 0-8069-0804-1
    1. Texture painting.   2. Emulsion paint.   I. Lipe, David, 1965– .
  II. Title
  TT323.A53   1994
  698'.14--dc20   94-7982
                                                   CIP

10 9 8 7 6 5 4 3 2

A Sterling/Lark Book

First paperback edition published in 1995 by
    Sterling Publishing Company, Inc.
    387 Park Avenue South, New York, N.Y. 10016

Produced by Altamont Press, Inc.
    50 College Street, Asheville, NC 28801

© 1994 by Lee Andre and David Lipe

Distributed in Canada by Sterling Publishing
    ℅ Canadian Manda Group, One Atlantic Avenue, Suite 105
    Toronto, Ontario, Canada M6K 3E7
Distributed in Great Britain and Europe by Cassell PLC
    Wellington House, 125 Strand, London WC2R 0BB, England
Distributed in Australia by Capricorn Link (Australia) Pty Ltd.
    P.O. Box 6651, Baulkham Hills, Business Centre, NSW 2153, Australia

Printed in Hong Kong

Sterling ISBN 0-8069-0804-1 Trade
           0-8069-0805-X Paper

Contents

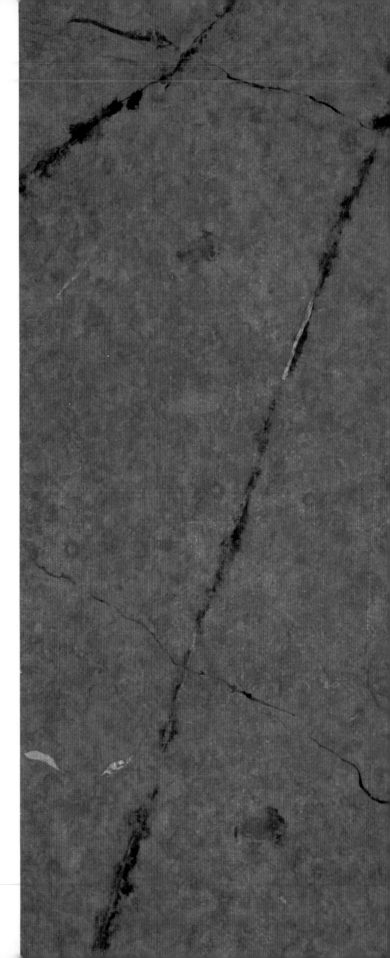

Introduction

PAINT IS COMMONLY USED TO DECORATE THE WALLS AND FURNISH-
INGS THAT SURROUND US. TYPICALLY, PAINT IS APPLIED IN A SINGLE,
OPAQUE COLOR—WHITE WALLS, BLACK FLOOR, RED CHAIR, ETC.
LARGE AREAS OF OPAQUE COLOR CAN DO MUCH TO AFFECT THE
PERCEIVED SPACE AND MOOD OF A ROOM, BUT THERE ARE LIMITS
TO WHAT CAN BE ACHIEVED WITH COLOR ALONE. THIS BOOK WILL
INTRODUCE YOU TO A BROAD ARRAY OF TECHNIQUES THAT GO FAR
BEYOND MAKING FLAT COLOR PLANES, AND YOU'LL EXPLORE MANY
POSSIBILITIES FOR CREATING TEXTURE, CONTRAST, AND MOOD WITH
WATER-BASED PAINT.

Decorative painting has been an important part of our lives for thousands of years,
from the cave paintings of ancient cultures to the faux finishes that are regaining
popularity today. Although fashions and materials have changed over time, the basic
idea of decorative paint finishing has remained the same: it involves the manipulation
of opaque and translucent colors to achieve a surface that seems to be more than
just paint.

A common use for decorative painting is the simulation of expensive or unobtainable
building materials such as rare hardwood or polished stone. Although these painting
techniques may be used to defray the high cost of more expensive materials, they are
also frequently applied for purely decorative or conceptual reasons. For example, one
or more layers of translucent paint can be used to create rich, mottled surfaces that
can give the impression of great age or simply set a mood. In any case, decorative
painting personalizes the surface to which it is applied; rooms and objects become
less sterile and industrial, creating environments that are visually exciting.

The beauty of paint decorating lies not only in its ability to drastically alter the look
or mood of a place or object, but in the fact that it can be accomplished fairly easily
and inexpensively by anyone with a little curiosity and patience. You don't need a
Master's degree in art or an arsenal of expensive tools to transform a dreary and ordinary room into a rich and personal environment. This book will help you accomplish
these transformations with the tools and water-based paints that are readily available
at your neighborhood paint and art supply stores.

A NOTE ON THE USE OF THIS BOOK

The greater part of this book is composed of "samples"—color plates that represent a broad selection of painted surface treatments. The plates are accompanied by detailed instructions that will enable you to reproduce all of the finishes easily. With most samples, color swatches are included to represent the colors of paint used for each step. These color swatches will make it easier for you to match the colors in the book since they can be compared to the sample chips or fan decks that you'll find at the paint store, or they can be matched with a custom-tinted paint. (Fan decks are manufacturers' sample books or charts.) The color swatches have been reproduced photographically from the actual paints used, but because of inherent differences between printing ink and paint, exact duplication of the original colors is not guaranteed. In most cases, however, an approximate color match will work just as well.

This book is intended to be a source of ideas and options, not just a pattern book. After reading it, you'll be able not only to reproduce the surfaces it contains, but also to use the techniques and information presented here to create your own unique designs and textures.

Plate 1. *A ragged finish can lend a mottled, antique look to walls, creating a personal, cozy space. The walls in this room were ragged with a rustic red paint mixed with glazing liquid. The same red glaze was applied again using a stencil to create a repetitive motif. Read about ragged finishes on pages 52 – 57, and about stenciling on pages 136 – 39.*

Materials

*F*ROM THE TIME WATER-BASED PAINT WAS INTRODUCED ON THE MARKET OVER THREE DECADES AGO, ITS POPULARITY HAS INCREASED STEADILY, AND TODAY IT OUTSELLS ITS OIL-BASED COUNTERPARTS. WATER-BASED PRODUCTS AREN'T LIMITED TO PAINT, THOUGH; WATER-BASED PRIMERS AND CLEAR FINISHES THAT EQUAL OR EXCEED THE PERFORMANCE OF TRADITIONAL PRODUCTS ARE ALSO INCREASINGLY AVAILABLE. NEW PAINT TECHNOLOGIES ARE RAPIDLY ALTERING THE MARKET, REFLECTING THE DEMANDS OF DECORATING PROFESSIONALS AND DO-IT-YOURSELFERS.

The advantages of water-based paint are noticeable both on and off the job. The most obvious benefit is the ease with which you can clean up afterward. Hands and tools can be washed with soap and water—no chemical thinners are required. Also, the odor of water-based paints is less noxious than the fumes from oil-based paint, and the "new paint" smell disappears readily, instead of lingering for days or weeks. And, since water-based paint dries quickly, it can usually be recoated sooner.

Other advantages become apparent after the job is finished. Water-based paints and finishes are more light-fast than oil-based products, so they won't fade as much in direct sunlight, and the clear finishes yellow significantly less over time. Additionally, the problem of storing flammable material is negated; rags used in the painting process can be laid out to dry before disposal, but even if they get piled in a corner, they won't be prone to spontaneous combustion.

Traditional complaints about water-based products concern their durability, vulnerability to humidity, adhesion, and poor leveling capability (which results in a tendency to show brush strokes). These complaints were valid in the past, but contemporary water-based products reflect the manufacturers' attention to these problems. Paint companies have been devoting their research dollars to the development of water-based coatings, and they have improved their products significantly in recent years. In many ways, today's top-quality water-based coatings outperform their oil-based counterparts.

PRIMERS

Primers are used to prepare surfaces for recoating; they seal porous surfaces such as new drywall, plaster, and concrete to provide a solid base for subsequent coatings. Some primers are designed to adhere to surfaces such as metal, glass, plastic, and raw wood. Water-based primers come in different formulations and vary from one brand to the next. Always read the manufacturer's description to make sure that a primer will perform the function you require.

PVA Primer

PVA (polyvinyl acetate) primer is a thin, inexpensive primer that is most often used to seal new drywall. Its watery consistency allows it to penetrate into the drywall's paper coating, ensuring a good bond. PVA has very low hiding capabilities and requires two to three coats for opaque coverage. It dries to a flat finish and can be used over existing painted surfaces, provided they are clean, dry, and flat in sheen. It's not recommended for use over oil-based paint or over water-based enamels. If you need a primer that will hide an existing color in preparation for a new color, you should select a more substantial primer than PVA.

Acrylic Primer

Acrylic primers are versatile and have excellent adhesion. The adhesion characteristics take two to three weeks to fully develop, however. The primer can be recoated within one or two hours of application, but the surface won't be completely cured and durable for several weeks. Acrylic primers adhere to such surfaces as old oil-based paint, wood, vinyl wallpaper, glass, metal, and other shiny surfaces. They are also fairly opaque, so they hide well. In addition to these traits, acrylic primers are good choices for surfaces that are stained by smoke, water, or the tannin present in fresh lumber. These stains tend to bleed through latex paint.

Acrylic Gesso

Acrylic gesso is found in art supply stores and is typically used to prepare canvases or paper for the application of artists' paints. Gesso can be used for home projects as well, but it tends to be more expensive than primers found in paint stores. It dries to a flat finish that can be sanded and is ideal for building up multiple layers to create a smooth surface.

White Pigmented Shellac

White pigmented shellac is an alcohol-based primer that is noted for its versatility and rapid drying time. While it's not a water-based product, it's included here because of its many uses and its ability to clean up with common, household products. Pigmented shellac starts to dry within minutes of application and is usually ready to recoat in a half-hour. The fast drying time can be a problem on large surfaces because the primer dries almost as soon as it's applied, making it difficult to avoid overlap marks. This can be alleviated by using a roller instead of a brush.

Materials

Shellac has excellent adhesion properties—it will stick to virtually any surface. It hides well, and seals problem areas better than any other primer. It's the right primer to use on raw cedar (which exudes tannins that travel through numerous coats of latex paint) and to cover sap, water damage, smoke stains, ink, crayons, or anything else that you suspect might bleed through the finished surface. This primer dries to a slightly glossy, nonporous surface that can be sanded. Tools can be cleaned with household ammonia or with alcohol. Denatured alcohol can be purchased at paint stores, but household rubbing alcohol works equally well.

PAINTS

Enamels

In this book, all of the base coats and all topcoats (thinned with glazing media) are water-based enamels. These paints dry to a hard, washable surface and are slightly glossy. Basically any water-based paint that isn't flat can be considered an enamel. Enamels are preferred for paint decorating because they dry to a nonporous surface. Flat paints absorb glaze coats and don't allow as much transparency as a base coat that resists the glaze. Paint comes in a graduated range of sheens as follows: flat, eggshell, satin, semigloss, and gloss. Unless otherwise directed, use low-sheen enamels (eggshell, satin, or semigloss) for the base coats and glaze mixtures in this book.

Water-based enamels vary in formulation and in character. One hundred percent acrylic enamels are the top-of-the-line finishes. Next in quality are enamels that contain a high relative percentage of acrylic resins. Lower quality enamels contain a low percentage of acrylics and are blended with vinyl compounds. For the purposes of this book, any water-based enamel will suffice.

Artists' Acrylics

When only a small quantity of a color is required, it may be cost effective to substitute artists' acrylic colors for enamel paint. These can be purchased in small tubes at art supply stores. They're available in a wide range of colors but may need to be altered for decorating use. This type of paint is very intense and rich as it comes out of the tube, and it may need to be mixed with white or black to adjust its value or with a small amount of its complementary color to tone down its intensity. Earth tones may also be required to tone down a color or to adjust its temperature. If it looks as though too much mixing is required, you may find it simpler to purchase the minimum amount of enamel at the paint store.

Mixing Colors

House paint is tinted with universal colorants, which are highly concentrated, water-soluble pigments. The palettes of the various paint companies may vary slightly, but they should include permanent yellow, permanent orange, pthallo blue, pthallo green, red oxide, yellow oxide, brown oxide, raw umber, red, magenta, violet, lampblack, and white.

These colorants can often be purchased in small quantities upon request. If you want to mix your own colors, use these pigments sparingly. Unlike artists' acrylics, which can be used straight from the tube, universal colorants are intended to tint a medium. They cannot be applied directly to a surface.

There is a limit to the amount of colorant that can be used in a can of paint. House paint is composed of universal colorant and a base, a neutral paint mixture containing a certain amount of white pigment. Light colors are made with a light base, which contains substantial amounts of white pigment, while dark colors use a base with very little white in it. Light bases shouldn't be tinted with more than one ounce (29.6 ml) of additional colorant per quart (.9 l) of paint. Medium bases will accept no more than two ounces (59.2 ml) of colorant per quart, and deep base mixtures should not exceed three ounces (88.8 ml) per quart. If the base becomes over-loaded, the excess pigment will bleed out when the paint is applied to a surface. The paint will streak and change color, making an uncontrollable mess.

Use the colorants sparingly to make slight adjustments to the colors you purchase from paint stores, or you can mix your own colors if you purchase the untinted base. If you mix your own colors, buy the deep base since it will allow you to create a broader spectrum of colors than you could obtain with the light base. (Light-valued colors can be made by adding white colorant to the base.)

A second—and probably easier—option is to let the paint store do the mixing for you. Choose colors from the manufacturer's fan deck, and ask the paint store to adjust the colors if they aren't quite what you desire. Before purchasing a color, ask the salesperson (or whomever is actually mixing the paint) how much freedom you have to adjust the color. Usually it's easier to make the paint darker rather than lighter.

Some paint stores offer a color-matching service that will allow you to have a color custom mixed to match a piece of fabric, wallpaper, or a color swatch from this book. This is useful if you're looking for a particular hue that isn't offered by the manufacturer. Usually, though, the spectrum in most fan decks is broad enough that you can find the color you need. It's also possible to ask for colors that are between two that the manufacturer does offer. Ask for color alterations in terms of quarter-strength steps (i.e., "make this one-half strength darker, please") since the formulas are easily divisible that way. In addition, you can have colors mixed that differ in hue from the manu-facturer's sample; color formulas can be tailored to suit your needs.

Glaze Mixtures

A translucent glaze mixture is created by diluting paint with water and/or a clear medium. This mate-rial is called *acrylic medium* at art supply stores and *glazing liquid* in paint stores. Acrylic media are generally used with artists' acrylic colors in combination with retarders and flowing agents, which are sold separately. Glazing liquids are used with house paints and already contain retarders. The purpose of a glazing medium is to dilute the paint, increasing its transparency and enhancing its flowing capacity, without causing it to become overly runny.

If your local paint store doesn't carry glazing liquid, you can use a latex paint conditioner as a substitute. Paint conditioner should be used sparingly, however, since it contains compounds that absorb moisture from the air, increasing the drying time of latex paint. If the enamel is thinned with too much conditioner, the surface will become reluctant to dry, and it may actually rewet itself in humid weather. In general, don't exceed a ratio of three parts conditioner to seven parts enamel, and be sure to read the manufacturer's instructions. Another option is to mix your own glazing liquid using acrylic medium and retarders purchased at an art supply store.

Glaze mixtures vary in ratio according to their purposes; a good starting point is one part paint to one part glazing liquid. Glazing liquid prolongs the drying time of the glaze, and water accelerates it. If a very slow drying time is desired, glazing liquid can be tinted directly using universal pigments. This glaze will dry to the touch within a day or so but should be left for several days before a clear finish is applied. To achieve a fast-drying topcoat, eliminate the glazing liquid altogether to create a *wash*. Paint can be diluted to any degree with clean water to create very liquid effects on horizontal surfaces. Washes must be clear-coated with an acrylic varnish because the paint is very thin, and the resulting film will lack durability. (**Note:** Horizontal surfaces, such as floors and tabletops, are subject to greater wear than vertical surfaces and should be clear-coated anyway.)

All of the glazes in this book can be altered to suit your needs. Frequently the glaze ratio is determined by the size of the project surface and the speed of application. Adjust the ratio to allow yourself to keep a wet edge while working; this is important for maintaining a uniform surface without lap marks.

Water-Based Clear Finishes

Water-based varnishes are becoming increasingly popular due to their many advantages over solvent-based clear finishes. They're easy to clean up, have minimal odor, dry quickly, and although they can yellow over time, the degree of yellowing is very slight in comparison with oil-based finishes. Acrylic varnishes are available in a range of sheens from matte to high-gloss: the higher the sheen, the harder the finish. Their rapid drying time requires a quick application, and two or three coats usually provide a tough, protective finish. Since these clear coats offer minimal yellowing over time or when exposed to direct sunlight, they're ideal over white or light-colored surfaces.

Apply a clear coat to wall surfaces in kitchens and bathrooms or in any room that gets plenty of abuse. Several coats of acrylic varnish are also required on furniture, counter tops, and floors.

Tools

Whether you're rolling primer onto a new wall or delicately tracing a marble pattern with an artists' brush, the quality of the finished product depends largely on the appropriateness of your tools. This chapter will introduce and describe the fundamental tools required for interior painting and for achieving the special decorator finishes that appear in this book.

BASIC PAINTING TOOLS

In many cases, the process of paint decorating begins with the application of a base coat on the project surface. To ensure a quality finish, you must have a quality base coat. Although most people know that paint is applied with brushes and rollers, it can be difficult to know exactly which type of brush or roller cover is appropriate to use on any specific project. Projects vary in size, texture, and surface material, and various coatings are best applied with certain tools.

Brushes

Brushes are used for precise, controlled paint application; they're typically used for painting cabinets, doors, trim work, and furniture. The main feature of a brush is its bristles, which are bound to a wooden handle with a metal band called the ferrule. Brushes are available in widths ranging from one to four inches (2.5 to 10.2 cm), and they are either flat cut (with the bristles cut square to the axis of the handle) or sash cut (with the bristles cut at an angle to the axis of the handle).

Always use a brush with synthetic bristles when applying water-based paints. Natural bristles react to water the same way that human hairs do: they get limp and separate into clumps. The synthetic (nylon) bristles retain their shape when wetted, so a synthetic brush remains stiff and uniform.

For each project, be sure to use the appropriately sized brush. Select a brush that will provide adequate coverage without sacrificing precision; i.e., use the largest brush that you feel able to control easily. For example, a 1-1/2-inch (3.8-cm) brush isn't appropriate for painting a door or a six-inch (15.2-cm) baseboard. The surface will bear excessive brush marks, and the painting process will be more time consuming than is necessary. A three- or four-inch (7.6- or 10.2-cm) brush would be a better choice. For a small project such as a picture frame or small piece of furniture, use a small brush. Large brushes carry too much paint, and the finish coat will drip and sag. Additionally, a large brush will feel clumsy and awkward on a small project.

Flat-cut brushes can be useful for flat, uniform surfaces such as flush doors and flat cabinet doors and drawer fronts, but sash-cut brushes are a better value. Sash-cut brushes are equally good at

Tools

flat paint application, and they're designed for painting surfaces such as window sashes or raised-panel doors, which have distinct edges or surface changes. Because the tip of a sash-cut brush is angled, many people find it more comfortable to use than a flat brush. The brush is held with a grip that is similar to that used when grasping a pencil; the hand and wrist are relaxed, and the brush is held at an angle to the project surface.

Because of their angled construction, sash-cut brushes are also very good for "cutting in"—a term used by painters to describe the precise freehand edge work required where adjacent finishes converge. For instance, a good painter can easily paint the moldings around a door without getting any paint on either the door or the surrounding wall. Another example of cutting in occurs when broad areas are painted. First the perimeter of a wall is cut in with a brush; then the body of the wall is finished with a roller. When cutting in, hold the brush so that its width is parallel to the edge being cut. Flex the bristles to give the brush a hard edge, and pull the brush along the cut edge so that the short side of the bristles is leading (see figure 1). Use the long tip of a sash-cut brush to cut into inside corners.

A good synthetic brush is tapered in cross section; this allows the brush to hold a lot of paint but keeps its working edge fairly thin and flexible for good control. To check the taper and, therefore, flowing capacity of a brush, bend back its bristles with your finger. Short bristles should pop out of the brush about halfway between the ferrule and the tip. On a good brush, the tips of the bristles are bleached. Bleaching softens the bristles and enhances the flowing capacity of the brush.

Figure 1

Rollers

Rollers are used on large, open surfaces such as ceilings, walls, and floors. A paint roller consists of a flocked, cylindrical roller cover on a rolling wire frame. Roller frames and covers are available in widths of three, seven, and nine inches (7.6, 17.8, and 22.9 cm). Nine-inch rollers are most commonly used for residential painting.

Roller covers

Roller covers are available in natural fiber (such as lamb's wool) or synthetic fiber construction. Always use a synthetic roller cover with latex paints. The depth of fiber on a roller cover is referred to as its *nap*; the appropriate nap size for a project is determined by the texture of the surface and by the type of finish that will be applied. For instance, a roller cover with a 1/4-inch (6-mm) nap is suitable for rolling glossy paint or varnish onto a smooth surface; a 3/8-inch (1-cm) nap is recommended for applying flat or semigloss paint to a flat or slight "orange-peel" texture; a 1/2- or 3/4-inch (1.3- or 1.9-cm) nap works well for medium-textured surfaces such as a "knock-down" texture or a light stucco finish; 1- and 1-1/4-inch (2.5- and 3.2-cm) covers are suitable for heavy textures such as "popcorn" ceilings.

A good roller cover has a dense nap, which allows it to hold a fair amount of paint. Additionally, a higher quality roller is less likely to shed fibers during use. In general, it's worthwhile to purchase a high quality roller cover since it will result in a more consistent finish.

Roller frames

A roller frame consists of a cylindrical wire frame that holds the roller cover. The frame rotates on a metal rod, which also forms the handle of the tool. The base of the handle is usually threaded to accept extension poles.

For two reasons, a roller equipped with an extension pole is much easier to use than one without a pole. First, the pole extends the reach of the tool; second, it provides leverage, which makes the roller easier to control. Extension poles are available in solid and in telescoping (adjustable) forms from two to 10 or more feet (61 cm to 3 m) in length. A solid, inexpensive five-foot (1.5-m) extension will suffice for most residential purposes.

Roller trays and tray liners

A roller tray is a shallow, sturdy metal or plastic pan. At one end, it has a deep, rectangular recess that holds the paint. The bottom of the pan slopes up from this recess to form a small "prep" surface, where the paint is evenly rolled onto the cover.

A tray liner is a thin plastic insert that fits into the roller tray. Tray liners are especially handy when more than one color is required on a project. It's easier to switch liners than it is to clean the roller tray between colors.

Painting Pads

Painting pads are useful for applying acrylic varnish to flat surfaces. These flat, flocked tools are either rectangular or angled (like a parallelogram), and are available in five-, seven-, and nine-inch (12.7-, 17.8-, and 22.9-cm) widths. Broad surfaces such as walls require the largest size, while the smaller pads are adequate for smaller projects such as doors or table tops.

Miscellaneous Tools

Masking tape

Masking tape is used to mask borders wherever a distinct paint edge is desired; it isn't necessary, but it's recommended for those who aren't confident or practiced in cutting in a straight line. The various types of masking tape and their uses are discussed on page 26.

Tools

Masking paper

Masking paper is available in rolls that are six, nine, and 12 inches (15.2, 22.9, and 30.5 cm) wide. It's typically used with masking tape to protect areas such as floors or wide baseboards that are adjacent to painted surfaces. If your project requires substantial masking, it may be worthwhile to purchase a masking dispenser. This machine consists of two rollers, which are mounted in line on a handle. The rear roller holds a roll of masking paper, and the front wheel holds a roll of masking tape. At the front of the machine is a serrated cutting strip. The tape is automatically applied to one edge of the paper as it's pulled through the machine.

Drop cloths

Drop cloths, or "drops," are used to protect large areas from dripped, spattered, or oversprayed paint. Three types of drop cloths are commonly available: plastic, plastic-lined paper, and canvas.

Plastic is sold in sheets and in rolls, and it varies in thickness from 1/2 mil (millimeter) to 3 mils. Drops that are 1/2 to 1-1/2 mil thick are too flimsy to walk on, but they're good for covering furniture or for masking vertical surfaces. Two- or three-mil plastic is sturdy enough to use on floors, but it's slippery.

Plastic-lined paper drops are effective disposable floor covers. This type of drop is used with the paper side up, which has two advantages. The paper facing absorbs drips and minor spills, and it provides a nonskid walking surface. Plastic-lined paper drops are fairly flimsy, though, and tend to rip easily.

Professional-grade drop cloths are made of canvas. They're available in a variety of sizes, shapes, and weights. Canvas is easy to walk on, and because it's relatively heavy, it's less likely to shift around under normal foot traffic. Also, it absorbs drips and minor spills. Since they're relatively expensive, canvas drops probably aren't appropriate for one-time use.

Empty paint cans

Paint stores will usually sell empty paint cans, although you may have to make a special request. One-quart (.9 l) cans are great for holding paint when brushing; gallon (3.8 l) containers are too heavy to lug around. This also protects the main batch of paint from evaporation and contamination. Pour off one quart (.9 l) at a time, and reseal the larger container. Since they won't rust, resealable plastic paint cans are also useful, especially for storing small batches of paint.

Caulk

Before painting, caulk should be applied to the seams between painted trim and walls. Door and window casings and long runs of baseboard are typical examples of places where caulk is needed. This simple step will disguise the gaps that can show when walls aren't perfectly flat or straight. Apply the caulk with a caulking gun, and smooth down the bead with your finger. Be sure to use a water-soluble caulk capable of being painted; avoid silicone caulk because it cannot be painted.

Spackle and joint compound

Lightweight spackling compound is intended for filling small holes and cracks in a surface before it's painted. Spackle can be painted over in a few minutes, and it won't shrink. It isn't intended for filling large holes or cracks, though.

Large repairs should be made with joint compound or heavyweight spackle. Large cracks in plaster walls should be reinforced with self-adhesive fiberglass tape, then finished with joint compound. Joint compound repairs may have to be applied in successive layers when filling deep holes. Allow each layer to dry before reapplying more compound. These patches can be sanded when they become flush with the surrounding surface.

Putty knives and taping knives

Putty knives are used to apply spackle; they range from one to three inches (2.5 to 7.6 cm) in width and vary in stiffness. Use a putty knife that is wider than the area to be repaired so that the compound can be skimmed across the damaged area in one pass. This way, the knife will ride on solid backing on both sides of the hole, and the patching compound will fill it evenly. Stiff putty knives are more useful for scraping than for spackling, and very flexible knives will deform across a broad patch. A good general-purpose knife should be fairly flexible and wide enough to patch small damaged areas.

Taping knives are used to apply joint compound. They're wider than putty knives, so they can easily bridge larger repair areas. Common sizes are six, eight, 10, and 12 inches (15.2, 20.3, 25.4, and 30.5 cm).

To repair a crack, first apply self-adhesive fiberglass tape, making sure that it spans the crack. Smooth down the tape with the edge of a clean six-inch (15.2-cm) taping knife. Use the same knife to apply a band of joint compound (or "mud") over the crack, laying down a coat that is thick enough to cover the fiberglass tape completely. To feather the edges of the patch, flex the knife against the uncoated wall, and drag the knife across the mud, maintaining pressure on the blade. Allow the mud to dry. For a smooth transition, recoat the seam using a wider knife, and use a sanding screen or fine sanding sponge to finish the patch.

Sandpaper and sanding tools

Sanding, while hardly a pleasant activity, is frequently critical to the success of a painted surface. In addition to smoothing down spackle, sanding can blend a joint-compound patch into an existing wall surface, knock down and smooth raised wood grain, or give a glossy finish some "tooth" so that it will accept new paint. There are almost as many sanding products available as there are reasons to sand.

Tools

The relative coarseness of sandpaper is measured in terms of its *grit*. Coarse sandpaper ranges from 20 to 60 grit; medium is from 80 to 150 grit; and fine is 150 or higher. This grit is applied to various backings. Light, medium, and heavyweight paper, open- and closed-weave cloth, and sponge blocks are a few examples.

Standard sandpaper is sold by the sheet in paint stores and hardware stores, and it's adequate for most purposes. Lightweight paper ("A" weight) works well on curved surfaces, while heavyweight paper ("C" or "D" weight) holds up better on flat work. Nonclogging paper is available in a range of weights and grits and is very useful for sanding primed or painted surfaces.

Two types of specialized sanding tools are especially suitable for sanding plaster and joint compound. Sanding screens are rectangular patches of fiberglass mesh that have been coated with abrasives. The screens are particularly effective because they can be shaken out when they begin to clog, and both sides are abrasive. These screens last a long time; professional drywall finishers may use only one or two screens to sand an entire house. Sanding sponges are small foam blocks that are coated with abrasives. They're good for feathering small patches of joint compound and for sanding curved or irregular surfaces. The sponges are flat but soft enough to conform to a variety of conditions.

Sanding blocks are tools that hold full or partial sheets of sandpaper; they provide a flat backing for the paper and make the paper easier to hold. Commercial sanding blocks are usually made of hard rubber and have small teeth that grip the paper. A simple sanding block can be created by wrapping or stapling sandpaper onto a small scrap of wood that has been encased in felt.

Tack cloths
Tack cloths are pieces of cheesecloth that have been impregnated with a sticky substance. They're inexpensive and are indispensable for removing sanding dust (and dust in general) from a surface prior to painting.

Wiping rags
Keep a damp rag handy to wipe up spilled or splattered paint.

Gloves
When using latex paint, heavy rubber gloves aren't required, but thin, disposable gloves are good for keeping your hands clean.

Dust masks
Wear a dust mask whenever you're sanding Double-pleated masks trap more particles and last longer than the less expensive masks..

Respirators

Respirators are designed to prevent the inhalation of toxic fumes that are given off by paints and finishes. A proper paint respirator has a disposable charcoal filter and fiber prefilter mounted into a rubber face mask.

Be sure that the filters you purchase are designed for paint and fume protection; consult a doctor for more information regarding product fumes and their effect on your health.

Goggles

Wear clear plastic goggles to protect your eyes from spattered paint, especially when rolling ceilings.

Clothing

No matter how careful you are, you're certain to get at least some paint on your clothing, so dress accordingly. Paint stores sell painters' pants, which are useful if you want to look like a painter. They also sell disposable paper coveralls and painters' hats, which will keep drips of paint out of your hair.

PAINT DECORATING TOOLS

The tools used for making the decorative surfaces shown in this book are generally readily available, inexpensive, and versatile. In part, this is by necessity; many specialized faux finishing tools are designed for oil-based paints and would be quickly ruined if used with water-based products. When you work with water-based paint, you must make do with ordinary tools that will suit your needs. Also, it isn't necessary to use expensive, specialized tools to achieve good results. Patience, flexibility, and modified disposable brushes will frequently provide the same finish. Avoid one-use tools whenever possible, and be creative in manipulating the basic tools of decorative paint application: brushes, rags, and sponges.

Brushes

In today's market, there is a staggering array of specialized brushes available; these brushes vary widely in price and intended use. Although specialized brushes are wonderful tools, and their special traits can make your work easier, they're expensive and aren't always necessary. It's the user of the brush, not the brush itself, who makes a great painted surface.

Flat nylon brushes

A standard three- to four-inch (7.6- to 10.2-cm) nylon bristle brush is useful for streaking and for creating various patterns and textural effects. There is a broad range of quality in nylon brushes, and it's worth buying a good one since its uses will be many.

Tools

Plate 2. *Left to right, tapered natural bristle brush, modified graining brush, natural bristle brush (unmodified), and synthetic bristle brush.*

Figure 2   ***Modified natural bristle brushes***

Disposable natural bristle brushes can be found at most paint and art supply stores. They typically have flat, unfinished wooden handles and blonde bristles, and they range from about one-half to four inches (1.3 to 10.2 cm) in width. These brushes are very affordable and can be modified in many ways to suit a wide range of needs.

For example, you can create a tapered blending brush by thinning one of these inexpensive brushes with scissors. Hold the brush in one hand, and snip into it with a pair of scissors held parallel to the bristles and the flat plane of the brush (see figure 2). Work back and forth across the width of the brush so that it's thinned consistently from one side to the other. Thin the brush until only a few bristles are the original length. Viewed from the side, the brush should taper from full thickness at the ferrule to a thin, wispy tip. The thick base prevents the brush from getting too limp, and the soft tip helps to eliminate choppy brush marks.

You can also make a modified graining brush quite easily by altering one of these inexpensive brushes. Simply cut the bristles to form a series of prongs. Since the prongs are made up of natural bristles, they will swell when exposed to water and will need to be trimmed occasionally to maintain the shape of the brush.

Sumi blending brushes

Sumi blending brushes are used to blend brush strokes into a painted surface and to create subtle transitions between areas of different colors. These inexpensive brushes, which are designed for

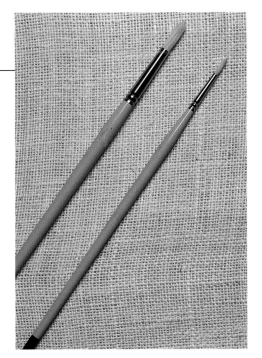

Plate 3. Top, *medium round artists' brush,* bottom, *thin round artists' brush.*

Plate 4. *A selection of sumi brushes:* clockwise from top left, *small, flat Chinese hake brush, medium, flat Chinese hake brush, and bamboo hake brush.*

ink washes, can be purchased at art supply stores. Before using the brushes, wash them under running water to get rid of loose hairs, and blow them dry to fluff up the bristles. For blending, use these brushes dry. It's helpful to have at least two on hand when blending so that when the first brush accumulates too much paint from the surface, the second can be substituted. These brushes are easily cleaned with water and blown dry.

Artists' brushes

The best selection of artists' brushes can be found at an art supply store, although most paint stores have a few for sale. Be sure to choose hog's hair brushes, which are compatible with water-based paints. These brushes are used for adding details, and the size required depends on the pattern you want to create. Don't use a fine-tipped brush to create long lines or to fill in large areas of color, and don't use a large artists' brush for fine linear work. Choose the appropriate brush for each job to avoid a lot of headaches.

Stippling brushes

Stippling brushes come in a wide range of shapes and sizes; they're dense-haired, blunt-tipped brushes that are used to apply an even, speckled texture to a surface (see figure 9 on page 61). A large stippling brush suitable for adding texture to a wall is usually quite expensive, but a round window-washing brush makes a reasonable substitute. Before using it, clean the brush to eliminate the loose hairs that would otherwise become imbedded in your surface.

Tools

Plate 5. These water-soluble crayons are useful for designs such as Wenge wood (page 112) and Perla Marina marble (page 68) that call for fine lines. The marks made with these crayons are easily blended into painted surfaces by brushing over them with clear glazing liquid.

Water-Soluble Crayons

Water-soluble crayons are artists' tools that are useful for creating linear patterns on a painted ground. They're used in this book to simulate veins in marble and grain patterns in wood. The marks produced with these crayons can be manipulated until they're wetted with paint or glazing liquid. This makes it easy to achieve a variety of patterns. Once they've been wetted, the crayon marks become locked onto the project surface.

Water-soluble crayons are usually found in a limited range of colors at art supply stores. Solubility (i.e., the ability to blend) varies from one brand to another. To test a crayon's solubility, use it on a scratch pad, and draw a wet finger through the resulting line. The mark should bleed and run easily.

Rags

Rags, despite their humble origins, are versatile tools for paint decorating. The best rags for this purpose are 100 percent cotton and lint free (or nearly so). Old T-shirts are ideal; they're soft and absorbent, and since they're well worn (or even worn out), they're relatively free of lint and fuzz. Cheesecloth works well too, but it quickly becomes saturated. If you use cheesecloth, be sure to launder it first to soften the fibers. Terry cloth offers interesting possibilities since it has a nap that will leave a stippled texture. New terry cloth, however, is loaded with lint, so use an old towel that has been through the wash several dozen times.

Sponges

Three types of natural sea sponges are commonly used in paint decorating: wool, grass, and cultured. Each type of sponge is appropriate for certain effects, so be sure to select the one that is best suited to your project.

Wool sponges

Wool sponges are soft and relatively uniform in texture, with pores radiating out from a central point. Because of their consistent texture, they have a high percentage of usable surface area, and their softness makes them superior blending tools. Wool sponges tend to cost two to three times as much as comparably sized grass or cultured sponges, but their versatility makes them worth the extra money.

Grass sponges

Grass sponges are also soft, and they're more oval in shape than wool sponges. The surface of a grass sponge has a nap formed by hairs growing in one direction. These hairs will leave a discernable, repetitive pattern, which could be a problem if a random, organic texture is desired. Unfortunately, these hairs become matted easily, requiring frequent washing.

Plate 6. Left, *wool sponge;* right, *grass sponge.*

On the plus side, grass sponges are significantly less expensive than wool sponges and are fine for small projects. It's also possible to find grass sponges that are relatively large, uniform, and short napped; such sponges are suitable for large projects.

These sponges were once living sea creatures, and each is unique, so it pays to select them carefully. Sponges vary in size and shape, and in price. The price is usually based on the size and type of sponge, but don't let the price fool you. A large wool sponge might be uneven in texture, while a large grass sponge could be fairly soft and uniform. When shopping, always look for sponges that are consistent in texture; they provide more usable surface area. In addition, select large sponges since they cover more area and will speed up your projects.

Cultured sponges

Although cultured sponges are used less frequently than grass or wool sponges for the creation of textured surfaces, they possess qualities that make them useful for some effects. These sponges are similar in shape to wool sponges, but they're usually a bit darker in tone and have a finer pore structure. Cultured sponges tend to be stiffer than wool or grass sponges, which makes them less desirable as blending tools. Their resilience when wet makes them good choices for creating stippling effects, and they're quite useful for replicating some granite textures.

Preparing and cleaning sponges

A new sponge should be cleaned before it's used for paint application since it may still contain loose particles and ocean debris. Rinse the sponge under running water, squeezing it out thoroughly several times. When it's clean, wring out the excess water—a sponge should always be clean and damp before you use it.

After using a sponge, you should always clean it before the paint or glaze has a chance to dry. An efficient way to do this requires a bucket of water and a few clean rags. First blot the sponge onto a clean rag to remove most of the paint; then swiftly plunge the sponge into the water, and reblot it on the rag. Repeat this procedure until the sponge is clean.

Basic Painting Techniques

*I*N ORDER TO PROVIDE AN ADEQUATE BASE COAT FOR DECORATIVE PAINT FINISHES, IT'S IMPORTANT TO HAVE A WORKING KNOWLEDGE OF THE ESSENTIAL TECHNIQUES OF INTERIOR PAINTING. APPLYING A BASE COAT MAY SOUND LIKE AN INCONSEQUENTIAL TASK, BUT IT'S AN ESSENTIAL FIRST STEP FOR EVERY DECORATIVE FINISH THAT YOU CREATE. THE EFFORT THAT IS PUT INTO AN EMBELLISHED SURFACE JUSTIFIES A FIRST-CLASS BASE COAT; THESE GUIDELINES WILL HELP YOU ENSURE PROFESSIONAL QUALITY AND LONG LASTING RESULTS.

PRELIMINARY STEPS

Before you purchase any paint, determine how much you will need. Calculate the area of each plane (wall, floor, or ceiling) by multiplying its length by its width. One gallon (3.8 l) of paint will cover 300 to 400 square feet (28 to 37 square meters) with one coat when applied to a smooth surface. (Rough surfaces require more paint.)

Next, decide whether you will need to prime any surfaces. A primer coat is required if the existing color contrasts strongly with the intended color. Priming is also necessary if the existing surface has an oil-based finish or if it's contaminated. Contaminated surfaces are those that have been tainted with a residue such as nicotine, ink, or smoke (from a fireplace or a house fire), which will bleed through a latex top coat. Finally, a primer is necessary on any surface that has never been painted; new drywall and bare wood are two examples. To determine what type or types of primer you will need, read about primers on pages 9–10.

PREPARING THE SURFACE

In order for paint to adhere, the surface being painted must be clean, dry, and flat. Clean a dirty surface with an all-purpose cleaner (or a solution of vinegar and water) and a scrubbing pad. Roughen a smooth, glossy surface with medium-grit, nonclogging sandpaper.

Before you sand a painted surface, consider its age. Paints manufactured through the 1960s contained trace amounts of lead, which is poisonous. Sanding a surface painted with a lead-bearing paint will suspend lead particles in the air and will contaminate the surrounding environment. Testing kits that determine lead content are available at paint stores. If the surface contains lead, then don't sand it; instead, prepare the surface by using an acrylic primer with good adhesion capability.

Carefully evaluate the surface, and spot-prime any areas that need to be skim-coated or patched with joint compound. Use a brush for small damaged spots and a roller for broad areas.

Plate 7. *The bold pattern on these cabinets was created by applying a clear gloss finish to a satin base color. To learn about sheen variation patterns, see pages 131–32.*

Small cracks and nail holes should be filled with spackle. Repair larger cracks with fiberglass tape and joint compound, and skim-coat the repairs where necessary. Where there are open seams between walls (or ceilings) and moldings, apply caulk.

Using a medium-grit sanding screen (or sponge), sand the repairs made with joint compound. Then sand them again with a 220-grit screen or nonclogging paper. In addition, sand any spackled areas that were overfilled. To remove any residue, vacuum and/or dust the surface.

Once all of the necessary repairs have been made, prime any broad surfaces that require it. Be sure to prime any areas that were repaired with joint compound. These porous spots will appear as blotches under the new coat of paint if they aren't sealed first with a primer. To apply the primer, you can use a roller, brush, or painting pad, whichever is most convenient.

Basic Painting Techniques

MASKING

Masking is an important step both when applying a base coat and when creating decorative finishes; it divides large surfaces into easily workable areas and produces crisp, clean edges. Masking off a project area minimizes stress while the surface is being painted, and it greatly reduces the amount of touch-up work required after the paint has been applied. This easy and worthwhile step should be included whenever it may be helpful.

Ordinary masking tape isn't suitable for paint decorating because it leaves an adhesive residue that is difficult to remove. The tape itself is often hard to remove, even after a short period of time. When applying decorative finishes, surfaces frequently must be masked as soon as they're dry to the touch; these surfaces aren't durable enough to stand up to ordinary masking tape.

Use medium-tack masking tape for surfaces that will receive additional paint or for freshly painted surfaces that are durable enough to remain intact after the tape has been removed. These surfaces should have dried anywhere from a few hours to a full day, depending on the thickness of applied paint and the weather (cool and/or humid weather will prolong drying time). Medium-tack masking tape is a fairly flexible tape with enough adhesion to prevent paint from bleeding under it but not so much that it can't be removed easily. This type of tape can be left on a surface for days or even weeks, and it will still peel off cleanly when the time comes to remove it.

Low-tack masking tape is usually stiff and papery. It has very little adhesion and won't stick to any surface that is porous or textured. It's ideal for glass or metal, though, and also works well on freshly painted surfaces that are dry to the touch but haven't fully cured.

Masking paper, which is available at paint stores, is a thin, slick product that comes in rolls. It's usually 12 inches (30.5 cm) wide, and it's useful for protecting surfaces from spills, drips, and stray marks.

Masking Large Areas

All of the surfaces that you plan to decorate should be isolated by masking the areas that you don't want painted. If you're applying paint to the walls in a room, mask off the perimeter of the floor with tape and masking paper, and cover the floor with drop cloths. Run a row of paper around the ceiling also, and tape off any moldings and other trim that will be affected. If possible, subdivide the larger areas to be decorated by utilizing such natural breaks as corners, doors, and moldings. For decorative finishes, you can also exploit the pattern itself to create smaller work areas. For example, striped patterns can be masked off and worked a few stripes at a time.

Applying a texture to a large wall can be physically challenging, especially when you're racing against the drying time of the glaze. To make large rooms easier to handle, work on opposite walls instead of working your way around the room. Use masking paper and tape to mask off the corners of the adjacent walls, then apply the finish. Masking makes it easy to work into a corner without worrying about creating stray marks on the other wall. When the first pair of walls is finished, take a break; then remove the masking from the corners. If the first walls are dry enough, mask them off and apply the finish to the second pair of walls. This system allows you to spend more time concentrating on the overall pattern instead of devoting too much attention to the corners, which can be time consuming. Remove the masking from the corners as soon as the surface has been finished. This way, any bleed-through that may have occurred can be blended while the glaze or paint is wet. If the corners are masked well, the textured walls should come together without a noticeable seam.

Doors, windows, and other architectural features also provide convenient boundaries for dividing a surface into workable areas. When the distance between the top of a door or window opening is fairly close to the ceiling, mask off one edge of the opening, and continue the masking tape up to the ceiling. If you will be applying another coat of paint or glaze, divide the surface at the other edge of the opening for the next coat. This will help disguise the small seams in the finish. If you notice slight value shifts at these seams after the entire surface has been finished, let the surface dry, and apply more glaze sparingly to the lighter side of the seam using an artists' brush or blending brush to feather the areas together.

Masking is an invaluable technique for creating linear or rectangular patterns such as stripes, checkerboard patterns, and paneling effects. These patterns subdivide the larger surface into small, workable areas with arbitrary edges, which make it easy to keep a wet edge and avoid lap marks.

APPLYING PAINT

Rolling

When applying a base coat to your ceiling, walls, or floor, you should always use a roller. (Rollers and roller accessories are discussed on pages 14–15.) A roller is not only faster than a brush, it also produces a smoother finish on a large area.

Before slipping the roller cover onto the frame to use it, rinse the roller under running water. Remove excess water by spinning the cover or by "jerking" it. Hold the cover at one end, and shake it out briskly by snapping your wrist. Rinsing the cover not only removes lint, it also minimizes trapped air in the nap, which can leave bubbles in the finish coat. Slide the moistened cover onto the frame, and make sure that it's firmly seated. If you have an extension handle, screw it into the roller frame.

Pour your paint into the roller tray, filling it to a point just below where the pan begins to slope upward. Dipping the roller partially into the paint, wet the roller, and pull it up the sloped portion of the tray. Then roll back down the slope to push excess paint back into the reservoir. Repeat this process several times until the cover is well saturated.

Basic Painting Techniques

The technique for rolling paint onto a broad area is the same whether the surface is a ceiling, wall, or floor. Beginning in one corner, use a sash-cut brush to cut in a section of the perimeter, as described on page 14. While these edges are wet, roll long, parallel bands of paint onto the surface. Apply the paint liberally, and work the entire length (from floor to ceiling if you're painting a wall, or from wall to wall if you're painting a ceiling or floor). Roll a few of these parallel bands, slightly overlapping the edges to ensure complete coverage. Then reroll the area lightly with an overlapping "M" or "W" pattern to eliminate the parallel tracks created in the previous step. Cut in the next section, and continue the process until the surface is evenly covered. If it's obvious that the paint won't cover in one coat, don't attempt to make it do so; let the surface dry, and apply another coat.

Rolling Ceilings

An extension handle is mandatory for rolling ceilings, even if you can reach the ceiling without one. The extension provides leverage and will allow you to apply long, smooth bands of paint instead of short, choppy strokes. Also, the extension will keep the roller and its drips and splatters farther from your face. To avoid drips, stand to the side of the roller rather than under it.

Rolling Floors

Using an extension handle will keep you off of your hands and knees and will help prevent your back from being strained. Thoroughly vacuum and dust all floor surfaces prior to painting. To minimize the chances of contaminating the painted floor with dust and foreign matter, close the windows and heat registers in the room, and turn off the furnace.

Roll the paint onto the floor in long bands that are parallel to the floorboards. Work from the farthest corner toward the exit door (don't paint yourself into a corner), and leave the door open to provide some ventilation. The open door will also help speed the drying process.

Wait a *minimum* of 24 hours before walking on a freshly painted floor, and treat the surface gingerly for at least a week afterward. (Walk in socks or soft shoes, and don't drag furniture across the floor.) Remember that horizontal surfaces take longer to dry than vertical surfaces.

Brushing

Brushes are used for areas that are either too small or too intricate to be painted with a roller. Read more about brushes on pages 13–14.

In general, paint should be used undiluted, but paint viscosity varies from one brand to another, and some brands may need to be thinned to a good brushing consistency. Don't dilute paint more than 10 percent with water; also, keep in mind that adding water will make the paint dry more quickly. To increase the flowing and leveling capacity of your paint, thin it with paint conditioner. Read the manufacturer's instructions to determine the proper mixing ratio, and stir the diluted paint thoroughly before using it.

Pour the paint into a container that is small enough to be handled easily, but large enough to accommodate your brush. Wet the brush with water; then jerk or spin the excess moisture out of the bristles. To spin the brush, hold it, bristles facing down, with the handle between the palms of your hands. Roll the handle rapidly back and forth in your hands.

Dip the brush into the paint until the bristles are halfway submerged. Then jiggle the brush slightly to load the bristles, and gently scrape the excess paint against the inside rim of the container as you withdraw the brush.

To apply the paint, hold the brush by the ferrule, with the handle resting between your thumb and forefinger. This may feel awkward at first, but it provides much more control than you can get by holding the brush with the handle in your fist. If you're painting with a sash-cut brush, paint with the width of the bristles for rapid coverage, or turn the brush on its side for precise cutting. In either case, lead with the short end of the brush. Use only enough paint to maintain the shape of the brush; overloading the brush will cause drips and sags in the finish. Don't starve the brush, though, or the finish coat will show excessive brush marks.

Tipping Off (Back Brushing)

In some cases, it's efficient to apply paint with a roller, then level the coat with a brush. This method, called tipping off or back brushing, works well on doors and cabinets. Roll the paint onto a small area—the paint must stay "open," or wet, long enough to be back brushed—and gently level the coat of paint using a three- or four-inch (7.6- or 10.2-cm) brush. Use just the tips of the bristles, and apply just enough pressure to erase the texture left by the roller.

Pad Painting

Painting pads are recommended for applying acrylic varnish to large, flat areas such as walls, floors, and table tops. (Read more about painting pads on page 15.)

Wash the painting pad thoroughly before using it, and shake out the excess water. After pouring the acrylic varnish into a plastic paint tray, dip the pad into the varnish, and drag it across the edge of the tray to remove the excess finish. Pull the pad across the project surface in long, slightly overlapping strokes. After pulling each stroke, turn the pad on edge, and lightly retrace the stroke to eliminate any bubbles in the finish. (**Note**: To apply acrylic varnish to small projects or curved surfaces such as table legs or cove molding, use a synthetic sash-cut brush.)

Color

THIS CHAPTER PROVIDES AN INTRODUCTION TO COLOR; A GENERAL UNDERSTANDING OF THE NATURE OF COLORS AND THEIR BEHAVIOR WILL HELP YOU TO MAKE DECISIONS WHEN SELECTING COLORS FOR A PROJECT. SUBTRACTIVE COLOR COMBINATIONS (WHERE COLORS ARE LAYERED OR MIXED TOGETHER) ARE FREQUENTLY HARD TO VISUALIZE; IT'S ESPECIALLY DIFFICULT FOR AN UNTRAINED PERSON TO KNOW WHAT TO EXPECT.

When you've learned about how colors behave when mixed or layered with each other, you will be able to select the colors required to achieve a desired effect. This knowledge and ability to plan not only will allow you to create the schemes that you want, but it also will save you time and money at the paint store. A knowledge of color will help you to meet your design objective and avoid trial-and-error decorating.

THE PROPERTIES OF COLOR

The color wheel (see figure 3) is composed of three primary colors: red, yellow, and blue. The secondary colors—green, violet, and orange—are created by combining any two primary colors. Tertiary colors lie between the primary and secondary colors. Red-orange and blue-green are examples of tertiary colors. Complementary colors are opposite each other on the color wheel (red and green, yellow and violet, and blue and orange are complementary relationships).

There is an infinite number of colors in the world, but any single color can be described in terms of four properties: *hue, value, intensity,* and *temperature*. The term hue refers to the essence of a color. For example, red, blue, pinkish orange, and lime green all refer to hues. Value refers to the relative lightness or darkness of the color. Any color can be made lighter by adding white, or darker by adding black. Intensity relates to the purity of a color. The intensity of a color fluctuates according to how much it is combined with its complement; an unadulterated color is very intense, while a color composed of complementary hues is muted. Temperature refers to the visual warmth or coolness of a color. Colors containing red and yellow hues are warm, while those containing blue are cool. It's helpful to understand these properties and to have them in mind when selecting colors for a project.

TRANSLUCENT COLOR

Latex house paint is formulated to be applied as an opaque surface coating, but when it's thinned with water and/or glazing liquid, it becomes translucent. Opaque paint coatings are solid and monolithic; they're unaffected by underlying colors. Translucent coatings, though, work like tinted veils—they add color to a surface while allowing underlying colors to show through. This creates variations in tone and texture; the finished surface relies heavily on what is underneath the glaze for its effect. The color chart in figure 4 shows how color behaves when it's diluted with varying amounts of clear glazing liquid and/or water.

When a translucent glaze is applied over a white ground, its color will appear lighter in value than the paint from which the glaze is made. This can result in a superficial or "cute" surface. For example, a rusty red color will change to a pink or orange tone. Colors that are frequently misjudged in this way are reds, corals, and yellow tones. Paint colors that are mid-toned will end up as pastels, and dark colors will thin out to mid-toned surfaces. For this reason, colors that range from mid-toned to dark are usually the best choices for glazing on a white ground.

This reduction in value makes it difficult to achieve a deep tone with only one glaze coat. If a deep tone is desired, build it up with multiple coats of glaze, or apply the glaze over a colored ground.

To get a rough idea of how a color will look over a white ground, look at the lighter versions of that color in a fan deck. Manufacturers' fan decks usually show paint colors in a monochromatic scale that ranges in value.

HIDING CAPACITIES

Each color family has a different level of *hiding capacity*. Hiding refers to the ability of a color to provide opaque coverage with a minimum number of coats. Yellow has the lowest hiding capability, and reds and oranges also hide poorly. A low hiding capacity makes it difficult to create modulated, visible textures with these colors if they are diluted and applied over other colors. Blues, greens, and violet tones hide well, which allows them to dominate a surface even when they are thinned to a glaze.

It's possible to balance a color's hiding capacity with its dilution; for example, it may be necessary to make a blue glaze thinner to prevent it from dominating a texture. To be noticeable, a yellow tone may require a higher paint ratio in its glaze.

SELECTING COLORS

When selecting colors for a project, first decide what the predominant color should be. This is the color that will register as the first impression when the viewer enters the room or looks at the project piece. Whether this tone is applied as a base coat or a glaze coat (or both), it will require the most paint of any color used.

Color

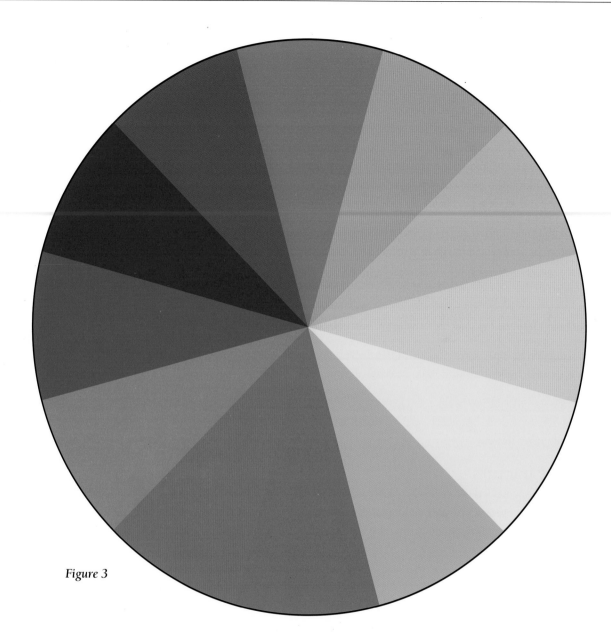

Figure 3

If you're having difficulty choosing a predominant color, think in terms of the color properties. Do you want the surface to be light, mid-toned, or dark? Should it be intense or muted? These questions will help you to narrow down the range of colors. Fine tune your choice by remembering how the colors behave when thinned to a translucent form. For example, if you're applying color to a white surface, order a darker, muted version of the color desired since color becomes lighter and more insipid when applied over a white ground. Finally, after the main color has been selected, choose accent colors to build a multitoned surface.

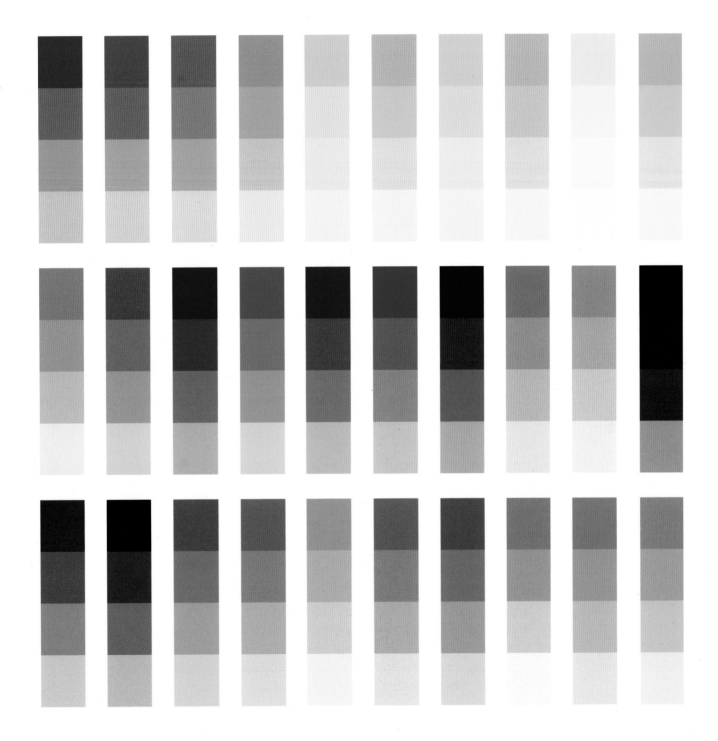

Figure 4

Color

AVOIDING MUDDY COLORS

Translucent layers of color behave the same way that colors mixed on a palette do. For example, a yellow wash over a blue ground will result in a green surface, just as if the colors had been blended prior to application. Muddiness is the result of mixing too many unrelated colors.

In general, remember these three rules: First, don't combine unrelated colors. For example, avoid mixing two secondary colors such as purple and orange. Second, use color combinations that are closely linked on the color wheel—colors such as yellow and coral. Third, use complementary combinations such as blue and orange to create grays when they are desired. These rules are effective guidelines, but they're not absolute.

Keep in mind that different application methods allow you to ignore the rules just specified. Muddiness is a result of color *mixing*. If one color is applied opaquely over another, mixing doesn't occur. The surface will appear blotchy but not muddy. White can also be applied to areas of a colored ground prior to the application of other translucent colors. This provides a cleaner ground for the subsequent glazes.

EARTH TONES

Earth-toned colors help to combat the "gingerbread house syndrome." Without earth tones, colors can create an atmosphere that is overly sweet. Earth tones add warmth and can often bring neutrality to painted surfaces. An umber glaze gives most surfaces an antique appearance. Ochre deepens and quiets yellow tones; a sienna glaze can age yellow and tame red tones.

COLOR CHIPS

When selecting colors for a decorating project, keep in mind the order and methods of application. It can be helpful to gather a group of manufacturers' sample chips in the colors that you intend to use, and stack them in the order that you plan to apply them. Overlap the chips to represent their relative importance in the color scheme, exposing the entire chip for the dominant color and just a narrow section of each of the accent colors. This process helps you visualize the project in terms of its color relationships and gives you an idea of the relative amounts of paint to purchase.

A FEW TIPS ON COLOR APPLICATION

Don't automatically apply glazes over a white ground. While a white base coat is effective for many treatments, it isn't always appropriate; it can limit the possibilities in some cases and force you to work a lot harder in others. If a dark, rich surface is the desired effect, start with a colored ground that will enhance the hiding capacity of your glaze.

In general, apply dark colors to light grounds. Light glazes over darker surfaces tend to look chalky. If a powdery surface is intended, then it's appropriate to work light-on-dark. This is easiest to get away with on those base colors that are fairly light. For example, a white glaze applied over a pastel color looks fine in most design schemes. On the other hand, an umber glaze applied over a slightly darker blue color results in a drab, chalky surface that looks bad in most situations.

Use the more intense colors as base coats or intermediate accent coats; don't apply them as final coats. Intense colors visually advance and can be subdued by the more muted tones in the color scheme, which recede and give the surface visual balance.

SPATIAL EFFECTS

Color relationships can determine the mood and atmosphere of a room, and they can also affect the perception of space within it. It isn't feasible to describe every color relationship and its effect on the space it defines, but it is possible to offer a general guide that should be considered when planning a color scheme.

The most important property of color, in terms of its effect on interior space, is its value. Light colors visually expand space while dark colors compress it. The temperature of a color also affects spatial perception; its influence is most noticeable on light colors. Cool colors recede, and visually enlarge spaces, while warm colors advance, constricting them. Third, the intensity of a color also affects space. Intense colors advance visually while muted colors retreat; however, the intensity of a color isn't as important as its value in determining spatial behavior. For example, an intense yellow will appear to be more expansive than a dark gray, but if the colors were matched in value, then the gray would be the more "open" color.

When colors are combined in a room, their interrelation has a great effect on the perceived space. Bold contrasts break up an interior space, reducing its scale. Complementary color relationships or sharp value shifts can produce dramatic effects. Interesting positive and negative spaces can be created by using doors, moldings, and walls as compositional devices. Subtle contrasts expand space by creating ambiguity. Subdued color schemes are achieved with muted tones or monochromatic relationships, which tend to unify a surface. One such approach is to make a subtle contrast between a wall surface and its moldings. This makes them read as one plane. Vertical lines such as doors and posts blend in and become unnoticeable, and the space appears uncluttered and minimal.

The same rules apply to horizontal surfaces such as floors and ceilings. On floors, color appears lighter than it does on walls. Light ceiling colors tend to heighten a room. Black is an exception to this rule, however; a black ceiling heightens a room by creating an ambiguous space or void. This illusion is frequently seen in theaters.

A FINAL WORD ABOUT COLOR

The properties of color noted in this chapter should be viewed as guidelines, not restrictions. Use them to assist you when choosing colors for your projects, but keep in mind that there are always exceptions to rules. Trust your instincts, and don't be afraid to experiment.

A Gallery of Project Ideas

Plate 8. Tabletops are great surfaces for creating fluid marble finishes. Because they are horizontal, they allow the use of thin washes, which meander and pool on the surface for very realistic effects. The method used for this table is found on pages 70–71.

Plate 9. With a little imagination, even a garage sale find can be reborn as an elegant piece of furniture. This table was first covered with a red base coat; then several coats of an acrylic gold paint were ragged over the surface. When the gold paint was dry, a dark charcoal glaze was wiped on to tone it down and to give the table an antique look. Finally, the side grooves and dark trim work were masked off and painted in with an artists' brush. The trompe l'oeil effect adds character to this otherwise simple piece.

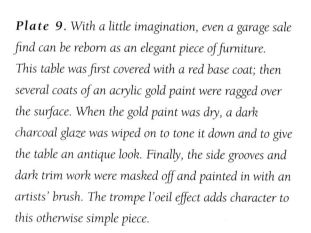

Plate 10. *Metallic finishes can be made to look weathered or older by using a patina. This table was first painted with a copper acrylic paint; the verdigris (green) effect was created by washing the surface with multiple coats of patina finish, which reacts with the copper in the paint. An acrylic varnish is essential to protect the surface.*

A Gallery of Project Ideas

Plate 11. *This simple pine armoire was transformed into a stunning and somewhat unorthodox showpiece. Read about metallic paints on pages 102–25; the spiral design is discussed on pages 122–23.*

Plate 12. A plain piece of
furniture can be transformed
into an elegant showpiece.
The repeated geometric
pattern used on this armoire
gives the piece a visual
complexity which belies its
simple construction. See pages
122–23 for instructions.

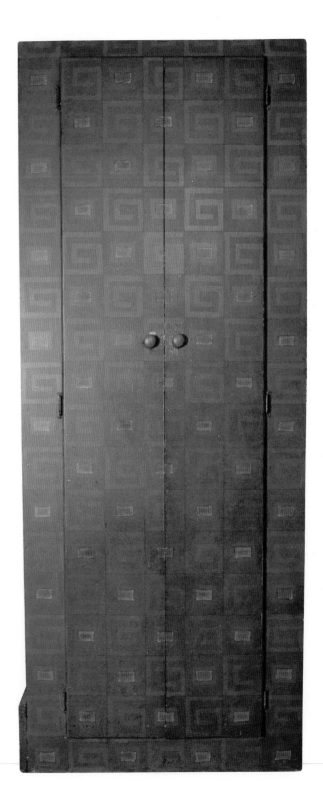

A Gallery of Project Ideas

Plate 13. Several techniques were used on this clock to achieve an antique appearance. The clock's face received a "crackle" finish, as described on page 126. The body was finished with a light blue base and a charcoal-colored glaze. When the surface was dry, the piece was sanded with medium-grit sandpaper to expose bare wood.

Plate 14. This concrete post-cap was transformed into an artistic centerpiece by applying a gold finish to its interior. Read about metallic finishes on pages 120–25.

Plate 15. *This flower pot was stippled with a sponge to emulate granite. More granite samples appear on pages 88–99.*

Plate 16. *The rich, blue malachite finish on this jewelry box isn't a replication of actual stone; it's a stylized pattern that gives an otherwise ordinary piece the appearance of weight and solidity. The instructions for stylized malachite are on page 86.*

A Gallery of Project Ideas

Plate 17. *To add color and contrast to drab interiors, create focal points of visual activity. This screen was painted with a dramatic striped pattern. For more about striping, see pages 127–30.*

Plate 18. *This lamp was finished with a loose, turquoise-green marble pattern that was applied with an artists' brush. For more marbling ideas, see the chapter on marble finishes (pages 62–87).*

Plate 19. *This elegant serving tray was created by gluing and nailing a piece of Masonite into a simple picture frame. The marble finish used on the tray was achieved with methods described on pages 80–81.*

A Gallery of Project Ideas

Plate 20. *Small projects are perfect for creative exploration. This chessboard has a sponge-finished, stylized granite base (see pages 88–99) and a black-and-white marble playing surface. Marble finishes are discussed on pages 62–87, and the checkerboard pattern is described on pages 131–32.*

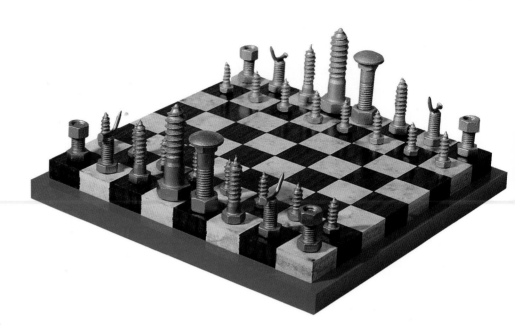

Plate 21. *A distressed finish can be achieved by sanding through paint and glaze layers to reveal underlying surfaces. This chair was painted with a gold base coat, then with a white pigmented shellac. The backrest was finished with a blue glaze. After all of the coats were dry, the entire piece was sanded with 100-grit sandpaper, which gives the piece an aged appearance.*

Plate 22. Picture frames can be customized to fit your decorative schemes or to harmonize with the images that they frame. This ornate white frame was first painted with an enamel base coat, then washed with a contrasting glaze. While it was still wet, the glaze was wiped off to reveal the undercoat except where it was trapped in the cracks and shallow relief pattern of the frame. See page 52 for a discussion of this technique.

Plate 23. Similar to the white frame in plate 22, this red frame was painted with a wiped rag finish. In this example, the darker color is predominant. The granite frame was created by applying paint with a sponge. The porous surface of the sponge emulates the crystalline structure of granite. Granite samples are shown on pages 88–99.

Surface Textures

THE SAMPLES SHOWN IN THIS CHAPTER CONCENTRATE ON TEXTURAL VARIATIONS THAT ARE MOST COMMONLY APPLIED TO WALL SURFACES. THESE TEXTURES ENHANCE SPACES BY PROVIDING CHARACTER AND ATMOSPHERE; THEY USE PAINT TO EXPRESS THE QUALITIES OF COLOR, NOT STRICTLY TO EMULATE OR COPY AN EXISTING MATERIAL. TONAL MODULATION IS ACHIEVED WITH TRANSLUCENT COLOR AND THE TOOLS OF PAINT FINISHING: RAGS, SPONGES, AND BRUSHES. THESE METHODS CAN BE APPLIED TO ANY SURFACE THAT CAN BE PAINTED, AND THEY ARE THE BASIS FOR ALL TECHNIQUES USING TRANSLUCENT COLOR LAYERING.

USE THE SAMPLES IN THIS CHAPTER TO SELECT A TEXTURE OR TEXTURES FOR YOUR OWN PROJECTS, AND USE THE COLOR CHAPTER TO HELP YOU CHOOSE A COLOR SCHEME. THESE TEXTURES ARE PROVIDED TO GUIDE YOU AND TO INSPIRE YOUR OWN IDEAS. DON'T ASSUME THAT YOU MUST ADHERE TO THEM EXACTLY; FEEL FREE TO EXPERIMENT.

BECAUSE WATER-BASED PAINTS DRY QUICKLY, THEY CAN PRESENT SOME CHALLENGES WHEN USED ON LARGE SURFACES SUCH AS WALLS. READ THE INSTRUCTIONS THOROUGHLY, AND PRACTICE ON A LARGE PIECE OF SCRAP MATERIAL IN ORDER TO BECOME FAMILIAR WITH THE SPEED AND RHYTHM OF THE PROCEDURE.

Plate 24. The walls in this room were finished with a rag technique described on page 54. The door panels were finished with the same green color, but the paint was applied vertically with a synthetic bristle brush (see dragging, page 58). The canvas floor runner was created by using actual leaves as templates, as discussed on pages 138–39.

Sponged Finishes

Plate 25

Materials

Base coat - Low-sheen acrylic enamel

Glaze #1- 1 part paint and 1 part glazing liquid (For a more translucent mixture, add more glazing liquid.)

Tools

Natural sea sponge

Clean rags

Shallow pan

Sumi blending brush

To prepare the surface for sponging, mask off any areas such as floors and moldings that are not to be sponged, and apply the base color. Pour the glaze into the shallow pan, and have some folded rags nearby for blotting the sponge.

There are two basic methods of application with a sponge, and both are *additive* techniques (i.e., color is added). The first method involves applying consecutive layers of glaze until the surface reaches a look of uniformity. The second technique is a one-coat application; small areas are sponged and feathered into each other to achieve a consistent texture. Each system has advantages and disadvantages, and each has its own look. Read the steps below to determine which method is appropriate for your project.

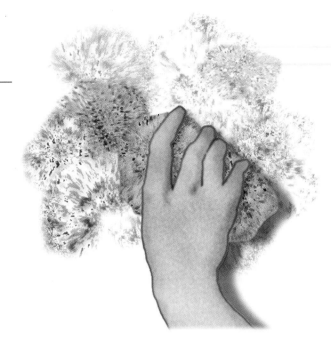

Figure 5

TECHNIQUE #1 (Plates 25, 26, and 27)

This technique produces a heavy, stippled texture. It's easy to do and can be used on a surface of any size.

Dip the clean and moistened sponge into the glaze, and lightly dab excess paint onto a folded rag. Blot the sponge onto the entire surface without creating any overlapping marks. Use just the "tips" of the sponge, and don't apply a lot of pressure. The surface should look spotty, with areas of bare wall showing through the glaze (see figure 5). To stipple into the corners, use a moistened sumi brush; the water will cause the bristles to swell and clump into separate "fingers," which will simulate the spotted sponge texture. Dip just the tips of these "fingers" in the glaze, and dab them into the edges and corners of the surface. Let the surface dry.

Reapply the glaze, paying close attention to areas that were missed in the previous coat (see figure 6). Two to three layers of glaze are usually required to achieve a uniform surface. Although this system requires multiple applications of glaze, each coat goes on quickly and easily.

Figure 6

Plates 25, 26, and 27 show the effects of using a white glaze over various different pastel grounds. In all three examples, the slight shift in value from the base color to the glaze color produces some subtle effects.

Sponged Finishes

Plate 26

Plate 27

TECHNIQUE #2 (Plate 28)

This method requires you to feather sponged areas into each other, which results in a subtler surface than that produced by the previous technique. Dip the sponge into the shallow pan of glaze, and dab excess paint onto a rag. Starting in one corner of the project surface, blot the glaze onto an area no larger than three feet (.9 m) square. To avoid obvious edges, this area should be organic in shape. Modulate pressure on the sponge to create subtle shifts in value, and be careful not to obscure the base color completely since that will make subsequent blending very difficult.

Feather the edges of the painted area by applying smaller amounts of glaze with diminishing pressure on the sponge as you work outward. The feathered perimeter of the sponged

area should be at least eight inches (20.3 cm) wide. Move to the adjacent area, and repeat this process to blend the new section into the existing area. Some small areas such as narrow bands of wall surface between windows and doors don't require feathering on their edges. If the area is three feet (.9 m) or less in width, simply work in one direction, and maintain a wet edge. (These small areas still need to be feathered into the main body of the wall.) Stipple into corners with a sumi blending brush, as described in the previous technique.

If more than two colors are desired to achieve a subtle, mottled appearance, remember to use colors that don't contrast sharply. Also, starting with a tinted base coat can minimize the need for multiple sponge layers.

Plate 28

Ragged Textures

Plate 29

WIPED RAG FINISH - SUBTRACTIVE METHOD (Plate 29)

Materials
Base coat - Low-sheen acrylic enamel
Glaze - 1 part paint and 2 parts glazing liquid

Tools
Paint roller and pan
Large, absorbent rags

Because this technique requires you to work into a wet surface, it's difficult to use on surfaces larger than five feet (1.5 m) in width. Although the glaze in this sample is more than 60 percent glazing solution, which prolongs its "open," or workable, time, it still dries too quickly to permit work on larger surfaces. It's difficult to blend a new (wet) area into a previously worked area without obvious overlap marks.

Apply the base coat, and let it dry. When the paint is dry, use the roller to apply a thin coat of glaze to the entire surface. Immediately wipe off the glaze (subtracting it) with a clean, folded rag. Use broad, swift motions, and reposition the rag to expose clean surfaces as the cloth becomes loaded with glaze.

WIPED RAG FINISH - ADDITIVE METHOD
(Plates 30 and 31)

Materials

Base coat - Low-sheen acrylic enamel
Glaze - 1 part paint and 1 part glazing liquid

Tools

Large, clean rags
Spray bottle filled with clean water and set to "mist"

Apply the base color, and let it dry. When it has dried completely, dampen the surface with the spray bottle, or use a very wet rag. After dampening the surface, saturate a rag with the glaze, and wipe the entire surface, working from the top down. If the surface begins to dry out before the glaze is applied, wet it again with the spray bottle. Be sparing with the extra water, though; if the surface gets too wet, it will dilute the glaze as it is applied. Too much moisture can even cause runs and drips, which are difficult to remove. This method also requires a small working surface, and it is best if limited to areas no larger than five feet (1.5 m) in width. Plate 30 shows the effect of wiping the surface once; in plate 31 the same blue glaze was used repeatedly until much of the white base color disappeared.

Plate 30

Plate 31

Ragged Textures

Plate 32

Plate 33

POUNCED RAG FINISH
(Plates 32 and 33)

Materials

Base coat - Low-sheen acrylic enamel

Glaze - 1 part paint and 1 part glazing liquid

Tools

Clean rags

Shallow pan

This technique is similar to sponging and produces a heavily glazed surface. Once the base color has been applied and allowed to dry, pour the glaze into the shallow pan. Crumple a clean rag, dip it into the pan, and apply the glaze to the project area with a pouncing motion. Don't remove the excess liquid prior to application—the glaze should be sopped liberally onto the surface. Keep the rag crumpled to create a noticeable texture. The thick application of glaze provides a predictable final color and a prolonged drying time, so it's easy to blend one working area into the next without leaving marks where they join. Therefore, this texture works well even on large, unbroken surfaces.

The textural differences seen in these two samples were achieved solely through the use of color. The violet base color used for the sample in plate 33 adds depth and richness not found in plate 32, which uses the same blue glaze over a white ground.

TWISTED RAG FINISH (Plate 34)

Materials

Base coat - Low-sheen acrylic enamel
Glaze - 1 part paint and 1 part glazing liquid

Tools

Clean rags
Shallow pan

This technique results in a stylized floral texture. Follow the procedure outlined in the previous sample, but apply the glaze with a twisting, repetitive motion. Since this method is slower than the pounced-rag finish, it's harder to blend work areas. Consequently, this finish is recommended for smaller surfaces.

A Note on Finishing Corners and Edges

When applying glaze finishes on a large surface, time is of the essence; try to keep a wet edge, and cover as much area as possible. Don't waste time fussing over the corners and edges of your project area. They can be dealt with after the bulk of the surface is covered. Here are two methods for "cutting in" corners and edges:

1. Use a sumi blending brush to stipple into these areas while the glaze is still wet. It may be necessary occasionally to load the tips of the bristles with fresh glaze.

2. After the surface has dried, touch up any areas missed by the rag with an artists' brush.

Plate 34

Ragged Textures

LAYERED RAG FINISH - ADDITIVE METHOD (Plates 35 and 36)

Materials

Base coat - Low-sheen acrylic enamel

Glaze - 1 part paint, 1 part water, and 1 part glazing liquid

Tools

Clean rags

Shallow pan

Mask off the project area if necessary; then apply the base coat, and let it dry. Pour the glaze into the shallow pan, and dip a crumpled rag into it. After blotting the excess glaze onto another rag, lightly dab the glaze onto the entire surface (see figure 7). When the surface is dry, apply another coat of glaze, paying special attention to the areas missed in the first coat (see figure 8).

In the sample shown in plate 35, two similar, translucent colors are combined using the layered rag method. When using similar colors, it's generally best to apply the more intense color (in this case red) first, with the other color (yellow-orange in this sample) glazed on top. Notice the areas where the red is partially covered by the glaze; a secondary tone, combining both colors, has been created. The layering of translucent color produces this third color, which is naturally and automatically harmonious with both initial colors.

Another way to utilize this technique is to combine complementary colors. Plate 36 shows an example using orange and blue. The orange glaze is applied first, followed by the blue glaze. Where the blue overlaps the orange, gray is created. These gray areas tone down the vibrant surface, making it easier to live with the combination of strong colors.

The success of translucent color layering relies on a broad range of opacity within each glaze layer. Try to create tonal variation with each mark that you make.

Plate 35

Plate 36

LAYERED RAG FINISH - SUBTRACTIVE METHOD
(Plate 37)

Materials

Base coat - Ochre-colored low-sheen acrylic enamel

Glaze #1 - 1 part sienna and 1 part glazing liquid

Glaze #2 - 1 part base color (ochre) and 1 part glazing liquid

Tools

Clean rags

Shallow pan

Medium-grit (80 to 100 grit) nonclogging sandpaper

First apply the base coat, and let it dry. Then use a crumpled rag to apply the sienna glaze. Once the sienna glaze has dried, use a rag to apply the ochre glaze, hiding most of the sienna with this coat. When the surface is dry, lightly sand it to expose some of the underlying sienna color.

Plate 37

Figure 7

Figure 8

Brushed Surfaces

DRAGGING (Plates 38, 39, and 40)

Materials

Base coat - Low-sheen acrylic enamel

Glaze - 1 part paint, 1 part water, and 1 part glazing liquid

Tools

Flat, 3–4" (7.6–10.2-cm) synthetic brush

Masking tape

After masking off the project surface, apply the base coat, and let it dry. Dip the synthetic brush into the glaze, submerging the bristles about halfway. Starting at one edge of the surface, brush on a vertical band of glaze. Then wet the brush again, and apply the next band of glaze, slightly overlapping the edge of the previous stroke. This will result in a slightly darker seam between the two bands. To hide it, lightly brush over this seam before wetting the brush for the next stroke. Continue this process until you reach a natural break, and to avoid lap marks, maintain a wet leading edge.

Pay close attention to the top and bottom edges of the surface as you apply the glaze. The brush is liable to drag less paint at the beginning of each stroke, which will create a light

Plate 38

"halo" at the top of the project area if all of the paint is applied from the top down. To minimize this effect, alternate between starting at the top and bottom of the painted area.

Plate 38 shows the result of dragging a mid-toned color (green) over a white ground. To add highlights, a second layer of white can be dragged over the green (plate 39). A more subtle color effect is shown in plate 40, where the two colors (green and umber) are closer in value.

Plate 39

Plate 40

BLENDED SURFACES (Plate 41)

Materials

Base coat - Low-sheen acrylic enamel

Glaze #1 - 1 part paint (contrasting color) and 1 part glazing liquid

Glaze #2 - 1 part base color and 1 part glazing liquid

Tools

Modified natural bristle brush

Mask off the project area, and apply the base coat. Allow the surface to dry. Next, using the tapered natural bristle brush described on page 20, apply glaze #1. (This brush allows the glaze to be applied with a minimum of lap marks.) Be sure to leave a noticeable amount of the base color showing through the glaze. Allow the surface to dry completely between glazes.

Now apply the second glaze. This glaze is the same color as the base coat and will blend easily with the base color left exposed in the previous step.

Plate 41

Brushed Surfaces

FREEHAND BRUSHING (Plates 42, 43, and 44)

Materials

Base coat - Low-sheen acrylic enamel

Glaze - 1 part paint and 1 part glazing liquid

Tools

Flat, 3–4" (7.6–10.2-cm) synthetic brush

Because lap marks are highly visible in this technique, it should be limited to small surfaces—those that are five feet (1.5 m) or less in width. Small rooms with natural breaks (doors and windows) or walls that are broken by areas of tile or paneling are ideal.

Begin on one side of the project area, and work across it in short, choppy strokes. Vary the direction of your strokes, but try to keep them approximately the same length. The brushwork remains visible, so keep a consistent rhythm to your strokes, and try to create a subtle but interesting pattern. As you work across the project surface, continue to load the brush to allow multiple strokes from each dip in the glaze. Maintain a wet leading edge, and don't stop until a natural break occurs.

Plate 42

All three of these samples were made using the same gray glaze. The tonal variations were achieved by altering the base colors. Plate 42 shows the effect of beginning with a white ground; a warm tone was used for the sample in plate 43, and a cool ground was used in plate 44.

Plate 43

Plate 44

Plate 45

Plate 46

STIPPLING (Plates 45 and 46)

Materials

Base coat - Low-sheen acrylic enamel

Glaze - 1 part paint and 1 part glazing liquid

Tools

Stippling brush (see figure 9)

Shallow pan

Flat brush

Clean rags

Mask off the project area if necessary, and apply the base color. Then let the surface dry.

A stippling brush is most commonly used to create a fine, speckled finish as shown in plate 45. This speckling can be applied in an additive or subtractive fashion; either method produces a surface with a subtle texture. For an additive speckled finish, pour a small amount of glaze into the shallow pan. Dip just the tips of the bristles into the glaze, and blot excess paint onto a rag. Starting in one corner of the project area, apply the glaze by pouncing the brush against the surface. Keep the area organic in shape, and feather the edges to facilitate blending.

To create a subtractive finish, first use a flat synthetic brush to apply a small amount of glaze onto the project area; then pounce over it with a dry stippling brush. Keep the stippling brush fairly dry by dabbing it onto a rag to remove accumulated glaze. Work small areas so that the glaze doesn't dry too quickly.

Another option with a stippling brush involves streaking, rather than pouncing, it over the surface (see figure 9). Move the brush in overlapping circular swirls to create a repetitive pattern (see plate 46). Work quickly in small areas to maintain a wet edge. Since this pattern is difficult to blend, it is not recommended for surfaces larger than five feet (1.5 m) in width. Again, this pattern can be applied in an additive or subtractive fashion.

Figure 9

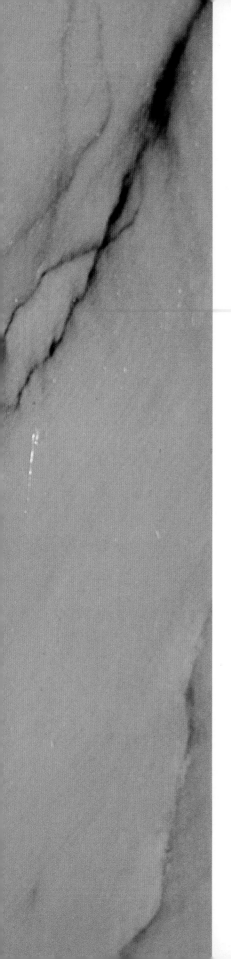

Marble

M ARBLE FINISHES ARE USED MOST FREQUENTLY ON SURFACES SUCH AS FLOORS, TABLETOPS, MANTELPIECES, AND PILLARS, WHERE ACTUAL MARBLE OR GRANITE WOULD BE AN APPROPRIATE MATERIAL. FAUX STONE FINISHES ARE VERY POPULAR, THOUGH, AND IT'S NOT UNCOMMON TO SEE THEM APPLIED TO SURFACES WHERE ACTUAL STONE WOULD NOT— OR COULD NOT—BE USED.

THESE FINISHES CAN BE APPLIED TO IMITATE STONE LITERALLY, OR THEY CAN BE USED IN A STYLIZED FASHION MERELY TO SUGGEST IT. MARBLING, FROM A DECORATIVE STANDPOINT, INTRODUCES ORGANIC FORMS, WHICH CAN CREATE INTERESTING EFFECTS WHEN JUXTAPOSED AGAINST RIGID PATTERNS OR SOLID-COLOR ENVIRONMENTS.

MANY OF THE FOLLOWING SAMPLES ARE REPRODUCTIONS OF ACTUAL TYPES OF MARBLE; A FEW ARE IMAGINARY AND DEMONSTRATE THE FREEDOM THAT YOU HAVE WHEN DECORATING WITH PAINT. IF YOU LIKE A PARTICULAR EFFECT BUT DON'T CARE FOR THE COLORS OF THE SAMPLE, DON'T BE AFRAID TO CREATE YOUR OWN INTERPRETATION.

Plate 47. Marble finishes can be applied to any surface. The interior panel of this door resembles a stylized onyx pattern found on page 78, and the white marble pattern on the casing is similar to the pattern on page 70.

Rouge Antique

BASE COAT
Rusty orange low-sheen
acrylic enamel

GLAZE #1
1 part rusty brown and
1 part glazing solution

Plate 48

Materials

Base coat - Rusty orange low-sheen
   acrylic enamel

Glaze #1 - 1 part rusty brown and
   1 part glazing solution

Black water-soluble crayon

White water-soluble crayon

Clear glazing liquid

Acrylic varnish

Tools

Natural wool sea sponge

Thin round artists' brush

Shallow pan

1. Apply the base color opaquely to the project surface, and allow it to dry.

2. Clean the natural sea sponge under running water to rid it of loose ocean particles; then squeeze out the excess water. Pour glaze #1 into the shallow pan, and use the sponge to apply it to the project surface. To apply the glaze, use a dabbing motion that is perpendicular to the surface (see plate 49). Allow the surface to dry completely.

3. Using the black water-soluble crayon, draw the veins on the project surface. The veins in this type of marble are relatively straight and few; they do break occasionally, however, and they should vary slightly in width (plate 50). The veins aren't permanent at this point and need to be locked into the painted surface. To accomplish this, dip the small artists' brush into the clear glazing solution, and carefully trace the veining. This binds the crayon's pigment in the glazing solution and keeps it from bleeding into surrounding areas. Also, it makes the veining more liquid and easier to manipulate. Clean the brush, and allow the glazing solution to dry.

4. Add the white veins using the white water-soluble crayon and the technique described above (plate 50). The white veins may be found within and alongside the dominant black veins, but they should occur less frequently. There should also be some small, scattered white veins perpendicular to the main black veins. Again, allow the glazing solution to dry.

5. When the surface is completely dry, apply a clear acrylic varnish. This sample shows how a clear, glossy finish can change the appearance of a dark color; the result is a richer surface.

Plate 49

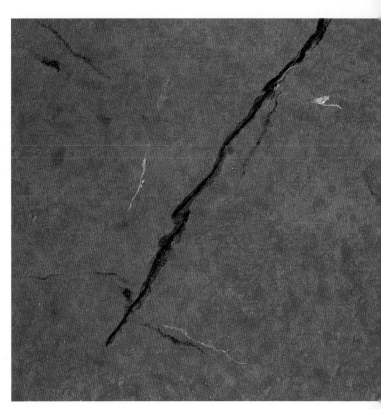

Plate 50

Imperial Danby

BASE COAT
White low-sheen
acrylic enamel

GLAZE #1
1 part green and
1 part glazing liquid

GLAZE #2
1 part yellow and
1 part glazing liquid

GLAZE #3
1 part light gray and
1 part glazing liquid

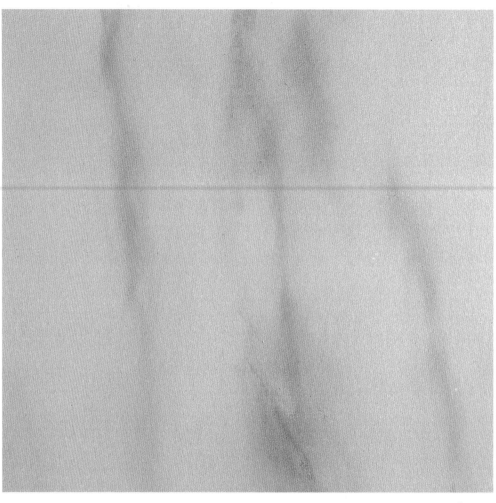

Plate 51

Materials

Base coat - White low-sheen acrylic enamel

Glaze #1 - 1 part green and 1 part glazing liquid

Glaze #2 - 1 part yellow and 1 part glazing liquid

Glaze #3 - I part light gray and 1 part glazing liquid

Acrylic varnish

Tools

Medium round artists' brush

Two sumi blending brushes

1. Apply an opaque base coat to the project surface, and allow it to dry.

2. Create the fine green veins by applying glaze #1 with the round artists' brush. Add the broader veins by dipping just the tips of the sumi blending brush into the glaze and gently stroking soft, flowing shapes onto the surface. With the second, dry blending brush, wisp over the veining to soften the marks further (see plate 52). Work small sections at a time so that the glaze doesn't dry before you can blend it. When the green veining is complete, wash the brushes and allow them to dry.

3. Using the technique described in the previous step, apply glaze #2 to add the sienna component to the green veining. Follow the general shape of the veins established in Step 2. The colors should overlap, resulting in a range of value and transparency (plate 52). After completing this step, wash the brushes and allow them to dry.

4. With a blending brush, apply glaze #3 to the entire project surface. This softens the veining, and you can use multiple thin coats to achieve the desired level of subtlety (plate 53). Allow the surface to dry.

5. The surface will look very soft and subtle after the previous step. To highlight the vein structure and add contrast to the surface, repeat steps 2 and 3 sparingly over the initial vein marks. The soft veins from step 4 will recede into the surface, and the new veins will advance visually since they aren't obscured. This interplay gives the sample the illusion of solidity and mass because there appears to be vein activity upon and within the surface.

6. Apply an acrylic varnish overall, and allow it to dry.

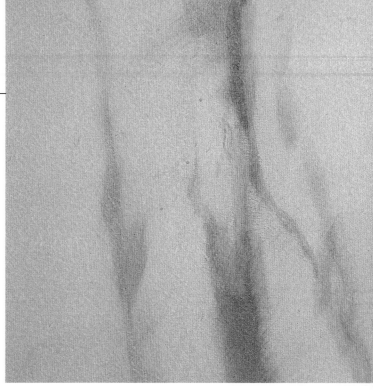

Plate 52

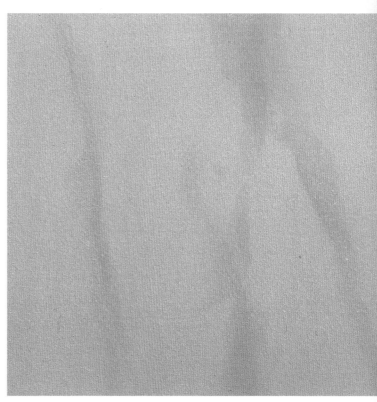

Plate 53

Perla Marina

BASE COAT
Light, warm gray
low-sheen acrylic enamel

GLAZE #1
Clear glazing liquid

GLAZE #2
Clear glazing liquid,
tinted to olive green

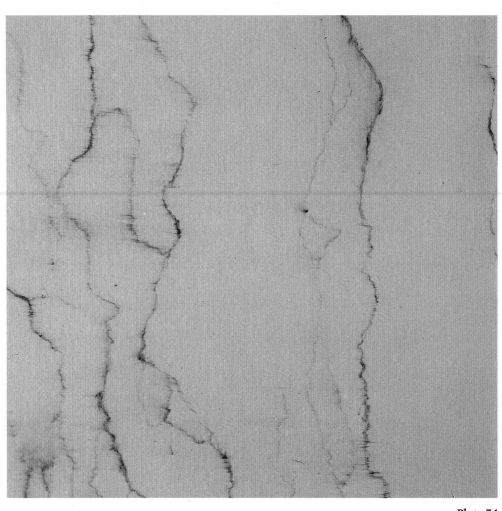

Plate 54

Materials

Base coat - Light, warm gray low-sheen
acrylic enamel

Black water-soluble crayon

Glaze #1 - Clear glazing liquid

Glaze #2 - Clear glazing liquid, tinted to
olive green

Acrylic varnish

Tools

Sumi blending brush

Thin round-tipped artists' brush

Clean cotton rags

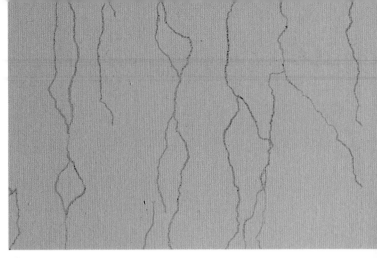

Plate 55

1. Apply the base color to the project surface, and let it dry.

2. After making sure that the black water-soluble crayon is sharp, use it to draw veins lightly onto the project surface. The veins should all move in the same direction and should branch and interconnect like lightning bolts. To make them look more realistic, vary the distance between the veins (see plate 55).

3. Dip the sumi brush into the clear glazing solution (glaze #1), and dab the excess solution onto a rag. Then gently wisp the brush over the veins, first perpendicular then parallel to their direction. This action blends and softens the veins, and it causes them to recede visually (plate 56). Allow the surface to dry.

4. Use the black water-soluble crayon to accent occasional veins, applying more pressure than you used in step 2. Then repeat step 3 over these veins. These selected veins are darker and sharper than those created in step 2, so they should advance visually (plate 57). Allow the surface to dry completely.

5. Use the small artists' brush to apply glaze #2 within and alongside the black veins. This step is subtle but adds warmth and color to the marbled surface.

6. Apply a clear acrylic varnish to the project surface.

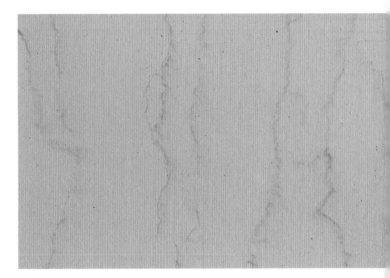

Plate 56

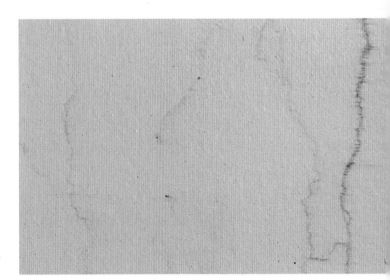

Plate 57

White Marble

BASE COAT
White low-sheen
acrylic enamel

GLAZE #1
1 part white and
1 part glazing liquid

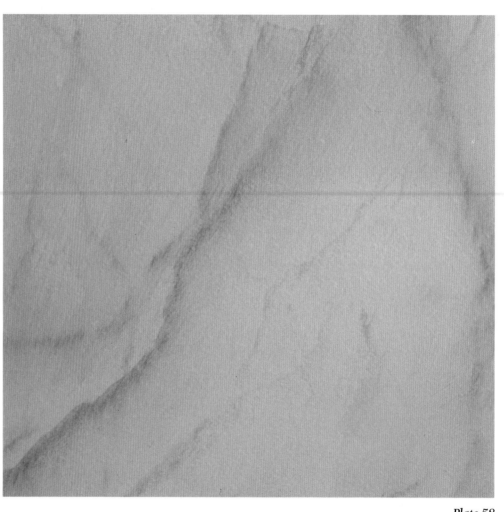

Plate 58

Materials

Base coat - White low-sheen acrylic enamel

Black water-soluble crayon

Clear glazing liquid

Glaze #1 - 1 part white and 1 part
glazing liquid

Acrylic varnish

Tools

Sumi blending brush

1. Apply the base color to the project surface, and let it dry.

2. Using the black water-soluble crayon, draw veins on the surface. Vary the thickness and darkness of the lines by modulating the amount of pressure on the crayon (see plate 59).

3. Brush the entire surface with the clear glazing solution, and soften the vein marks by brushing over them repeatedly (plate 60). Wash out the brush, and allow the surface to dry.

4. With the blending brush, apply a coat of white glaze (glaze #1) over the entire surface. Alternate the direction of your brush strokes to avoid obvious streaking.

5. When the surface is completely dry, apply an acrylic varnish.

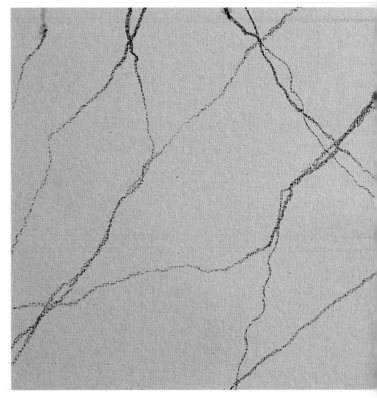

Plate 59

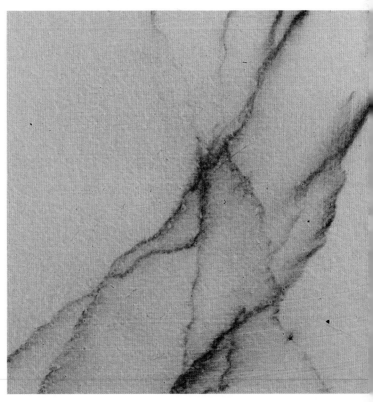

Plate 60

Sunflower

Plate 61

BASE COAT
White low-sheen
acrylic enamel

GLAZE #1
1 part sienna and
1 part glazing liquid

GLAZE #2
1 part light gray and
1 part glazing liquid

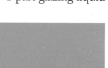

GLAZE #3
1 part yellow ochre and
1 part glazing liquid

GLAZE #4
1 part white and
1 part glazing liquid

Materials

Base coat - White low-sheen acrylic enamel

Glaze #1 - 1 part sienna and 1 part
glazing liquid

Glaze #2 - 1 part light gray and 1 part
glazing liquid

Glaze #3 - 1 part yellow ochre and 1 part
glazing liquid

Glaze #4 - 1 part white and 1 part
glazing liquid

Acrylic varnish

Tools

Two sumi blending brushes

Thin round-tipped artists' brush

Hair dryer

1. Apply the base color to the project surface, and let it dry completely.

2. To create the background vein structure, apply the sienna glaze (glaze #1) with both sumi blending brushes. Dip just the tips of the bristles of the first brush into the glaze, and gently wisp it onto the surface to create soft, flowing veins. Immediately follow with the second (clean) blending brush; lightly brush over the marks to further soften and blend them (see plate 62). Work one vein at a time so that the glaze will not set before it can be blended. Blending and softening are best accomplished with dry brushes, so it may be necessary to clean the brushes and dry them frequently with the hair dryer. Allow the surface to dry.

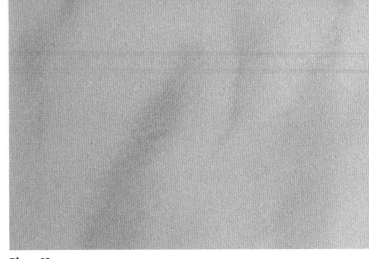

Plate 62

3. Use one of the blending brushes to apply the gray glaze (glaze #2) to the entire surface (plate 63). Let the surface dry.

4. Using the thin artists' brush, paint the surface veining onto the underlying structure developed in step 2. Create the veins with the sienna glaze (glaze #1), and highlight them with the ochre (glaze #3) and white (glaze #4) glazes. It's important that these veins vary in size, width, intensity, and direction. To achieve these effects, pay close attention to your brushwork. The quality of line can be modulated by applying different degrees of pressure to the brush and by varying the amount of glaze loaded on the bristles. Additionally, if you twist the brush while dragging it, then you can create looser marks with the feathered ends (plate 64). Allow the surface to dry.

Plate 63

5. Apply another thin coat of gray glaze (glaze #2). Lightly feather the glaze over the dark veins to avoid obscuring them.

6. When the project surface is dry, apply an acrylic varnish.

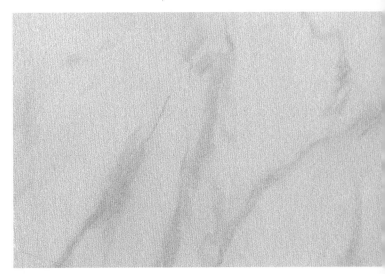

Plate 64

Noir Cihique

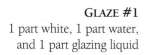

BASE COAT
Black low-sheen
acrylic enamel

GLAZE #1
1 part white, 1 part water,
and 1 part glazing liquid

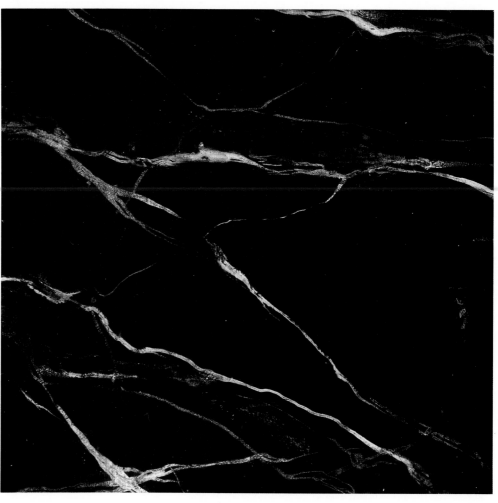

Plate 65

Materials

Base coat - Black low-sheen acrylic enamel

Glaze #1 - 1 part white, 1 part water, and 1
    part glazing liquid

Acrylic varnish

Tools

Thin round-tipped artists' brush

Clean cotton rags

1. Apply the base color to the project surface, making sure to give opaque coverage. Allow the surface to dry.

2. Create the white veins by using the thin artists' brush to apply glaze #1. The veins should vary dramatically in width, from broad fans to hairline cracks (see plate 66). Wash out the brush, and allow the surface to dry.

Note: Working on a black background makes it difficult to conceal mistakes. Any attempted erasure or alteration will leave a chalky blur. If this occurs, the blur can be corrected by washing the affected area with a black glaze (1 part black and 1 part glazing solution) after the surface is dry.

3. Dampen a clean cotton rag, and dip one corner into the white glaze. Blot the excess liquid onto another rag using a good deal of pressure; only a minimal amount of glaze should remain on the rag used for application. Lightly wipe and dab the rag onto the project surface to create a cloudy texture, especially among the veins. If the contrast is too great, apply a black wash over the affected area (see the note above). Then allow the surface to dry.

4. Apply an acrylic varnish.

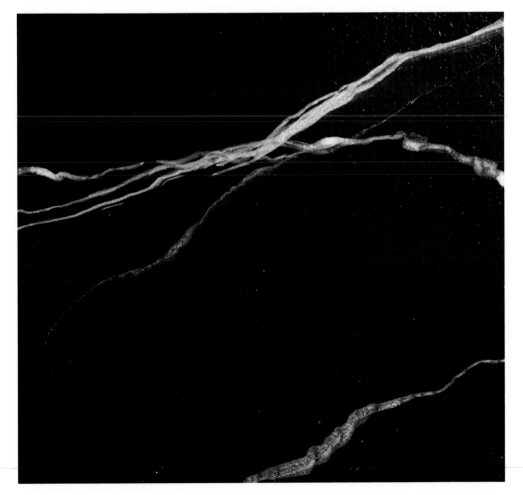

Plate 66

Yellow Marble

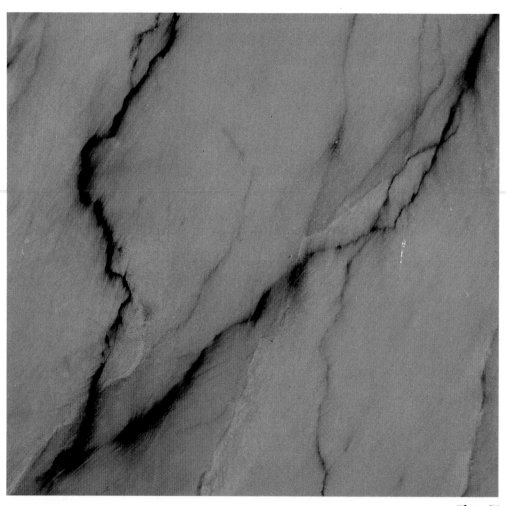

Plate 67

Materials

Base coat - Yellow low-sheen acrylic enamel

Glaze #1 - 1 part light yellow and 1 part glazing liquid

Glaze #2 - 1 part yellow (base coat color) and 1 part glazing liquid

Black water-soluble crayon

Acrylic varnish

Tools

Sumi blending brush

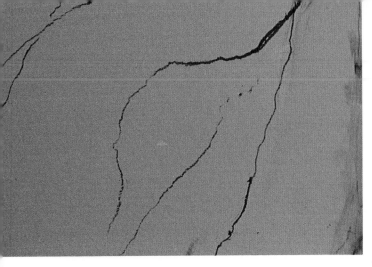

Plate 68

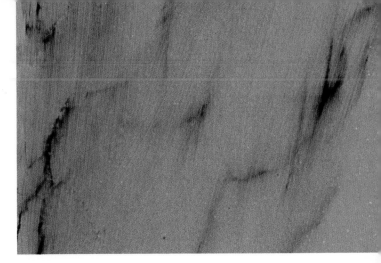

Plate 69

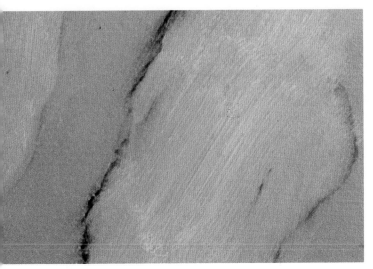

Plate 70

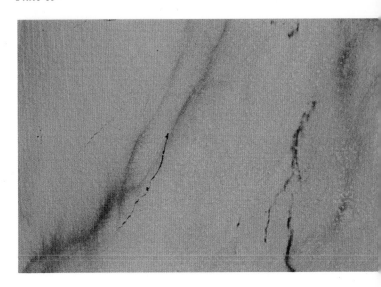

Plate 71

1. Apply at least two coats of the base color to the project surface. For good results, opaque coverage is required.

2. Using the black water-soluble crayon, draw veins that vary in width and direction (see plate 68).

3. Dip the sumi blending brush into the clear glazing solution, and lightly wisp it over the project surface. This softens the vein marks and locks them onto the painted surface (plate 69). Wash the brush, and allow the surface to dry.

4. With the blending brush, apply glaze #1 to selected areas of the surface. Use the veins as boundaries for these areas, and vary the level of opacity within them to give the sur-face added depth and character (plate 70). Clean the brush, and let the project surface dry completely.

5. Using the sumi brush, apply a thin coat of glaze #2 over the lightened areas laid down in the previous step. Since this glaze is the same color as the base coat, it will blend the lighter areas into the background (plate 71). Again, wash out the brush, and let the surface dry.

6. With the water-soluble crayon, emphasize a few of the veins created in step 2; then lightly wisp them with clear glazing solution to bind the pigment.

7. When the project surface is dry, apply an acrylic varnish.

Onyx

BASE COAT
White

GLAZE #1
1 part yellow ochre and
1 part glazing liquid

GLAZE #2
1 part white and
1 part glazing liquid

GLAZE #3
1 part pink and
1 part glazing liquid

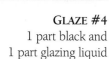

GLAZE #4
1 part black and
1 part glazing liquid

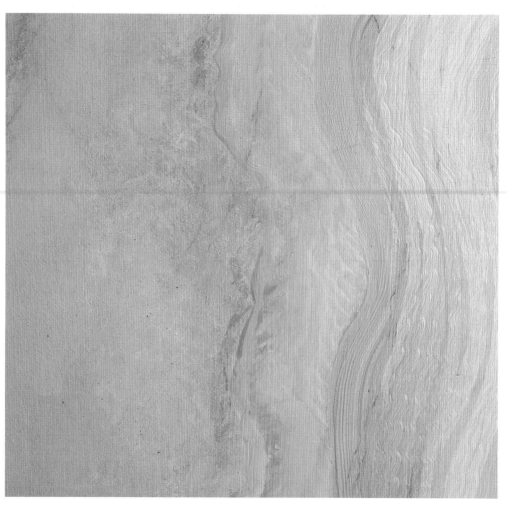

Plate 72

Materials

Base coat - White

Glaze #1 - 1 part yellow ochre and 1 part
glazing liquid

Glaze #2 - 1 part white and 1 part
glazing liquid

Glaze #3 - 1 part pink and 1 part
glazing liquid

Glaze #4 - 1 part black and 1 part
glazing liquid

Acrylic varnish

Tools

Clean cotton rags

Shallow pan

Sumi blending brush

Medium round-tipped artists' brush

Plate 73

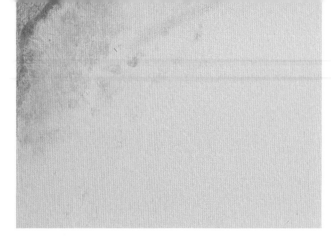

Plate 74

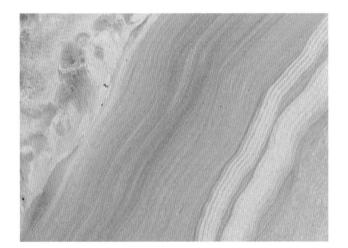

Plate 75

Plate 76

1. Apply the base color to the project surface, and let it dry.

2. Onyx is characterized by blotchy crystalline areas surrounded by curving, striated bands of color. To mimic these, begin by using a crumpled rag to dab the ochre glaze (glaze #1) onto the project surface. Apply a loose, somewhat circular area of glaze, and follow it with a second band, loosely overlapping the previous glaze. If done properly, this will result in a dark seam, or ring, between the two lighter areas (see plate 73).

3. Use another rag loaded with white glaze (glaze #2) to subdue most of the ochre laid down in the previous step. Dab the white glaze over the wet ochre glaze up to, but not onto, the darker ring. Alternate between glaze #1 and #2 to create concentric organic shapes with a broad range of tonal variation. The surface should look something like a topographic map, or ocean tides seen in an aerial view (plate 74).

4. Using the blending brush, apply the ochre glaze (glaze #1) in a wide band that meets the edge of the area created in the previous step. Then use the tip of a dampened rag to subtract thin ribbons of glaze from this band (plate 75). Continue to alternate steps 2, 3, and 4, applying all glazes wet-on-wet, until the surface is covered. When the surface is covered, let it dry completely.

5. When the surface is dry, apply secondary veins of glazes #3 and #4 with a medium artists' brush, and allow them to dry (plate 76).

6. To subdue the surface, use the blending brush to apply the white glaze liberally over much of the surface. Follow the established rhythms, and leave occasional areas bare. The intermittent hints of rich color keep the surface from becoming pasty.

7. When the surface has dried, apply an acrylic varnish.

Ruivina Clara

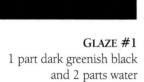

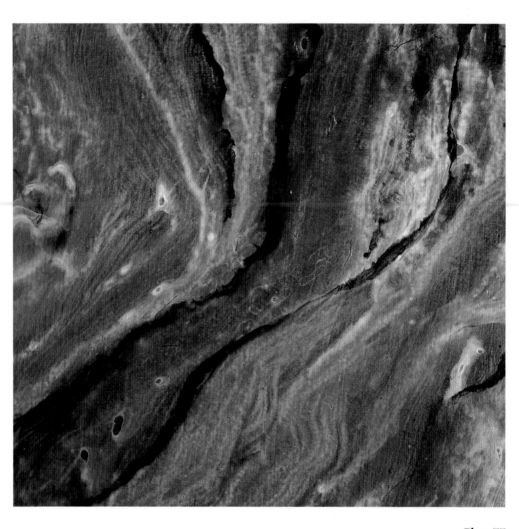

Plate 77

Materials

Base coat - White low-sheen acrylic enamel

Glaze #1 - 1 part dark greenish black and 2 parts water

Glaze #2 - 1 part white and 2 parts water

Acrylic varnish

Note: Because the glazes used in this pattern are highly diluted, they're suitable only for applying to horizontal surfaces.

Tools

Sumi blending brush

Medium round artists' brush

1. Apply the base color to the project surface. Allow it to dry.

2. Using the sumi blending brush, apply a liberal wash of glaze #1. The brush strokes should all flow in the same direction, but should not be absolutely parallel. Overlap the brush strokes to achieve tonal variation (see plate 78). Allow the surface to dry, and wash out the blending brush. Retain glaze #1 for use in step 4.

3. Wet the project surface with a damp rag, and use the blending brush to apply glaze #2 to the project surface. Follow the brush strokes laid down in step 2, but be sure to allow "crevices" of the underlying dark glaze to remain.

Dab the project surface with a loaded brush—the surface should be very wet—and allow this glaze to evaporate. This will create the mottled, organic "pooling" that is typical of this marble (plate 79). Allow the surface to dry.

4. With the artists' brush, apply glaze #1 to emphasize the grain pattern established in the previous steps, and highlight any detail that may have been obscured by the light-colored wash of step 3. Allow the surface to dry.

5. It's absolutely necessary in this case to apply an acrylic varnish.

Plate 78

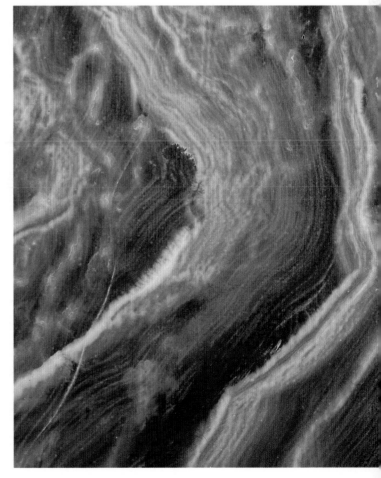

Plate 79

Grigio Romano

BASE COAT
Dark green low-sheen
acrylic enamel

GLAZE #1
1 part black and
2 parts water

GLAZE #2
1 part light gray and
2 parts water

GLAZE #3
1 part yellow ochre and
2 parts water

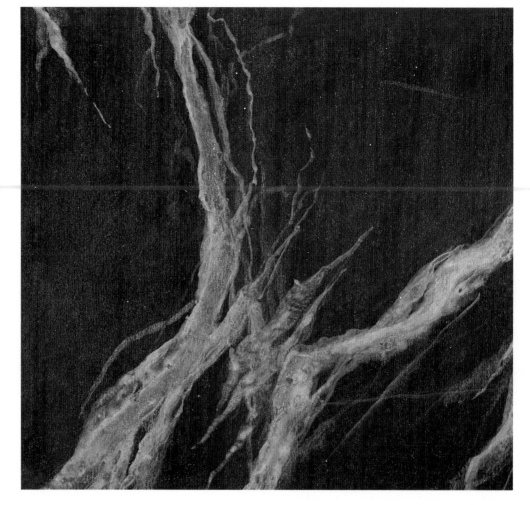

Plate 80

Materials

Base coat - Dark green low-sheen
    acrylic enamel

Glaze #1 - 1 part black and 2 parts water

Glaze #2 - 1 part light gray and 2 parts water

Glaze #3 - 1 part yellow ochre and 2
    parts water

Acrylic varnish

Note: Because the glazes used in this pattern are highly diluted, they're suitable only for applying to horizontal surfaces.

Tools

Broad round artists' brush

Thin round artists' brush

Clean cotton rags

Plate 81

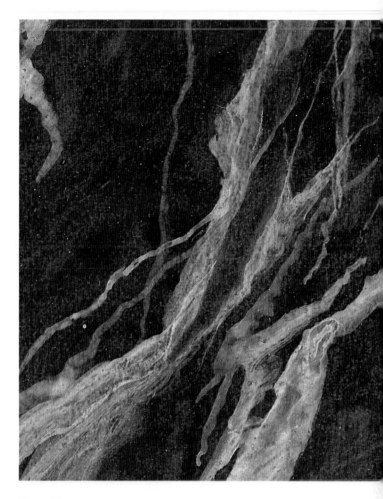

Plate 82

1. Apply the base color to the project surface, making sure that you have opaque coverage, and let the surface dry.

2. Load the broad artists' brush liberally with the black glaze (glaze #1). Press the brush onto the project surface until the bristles fan out; then twist and drag it over the surface to create an organic field (see plate 81). Clean the brush, and allow the surface to dry.

3. The veins in this type of marble vary greatly in size and shape. First create the larger veins by applying glaze #2 with the broad round artists' brush. These veins should be fluid and should have a high degree of tonal variation. To achieve this effect, load the broad brush, and jiggle it as you drag it across the painted surface. Allow the glaze to

collect on the surface, where it will pool and separate. Now use the thin artists' brush to apply the smaller veins, which should cluster together in some places and drift away separately in others. Cross the finer veins over the larger ones to add depth and contrast to the design (plate 82). Wash the brushes, and allow the surface to dry.

4. Highlight the veins with glaze #3. When you add these accents, use a fairly dry brush (dab the excess glaze onto a clean rag before applying the glaze to the project surface). Only a few highlights are required, so add them sparingly. Allow the surface to dry.

5. Apply an acrylic varnish.

Verde Viana Escuro

BASE COAT
White low-sheen
acrylic enamel

GLAZE #1
1 part green and
2 parts water

GLAZE #2
1 part sienna and
2 parts water

GLAZE #3
1 part black and
1 part water

GLAZE #4
1 part light green and
1 part glazing liquid

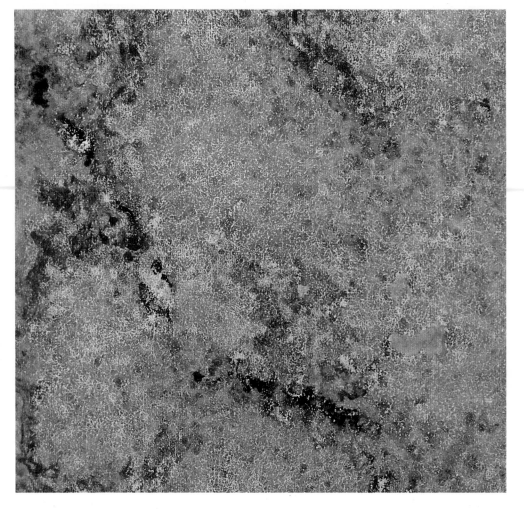

Plate 83

Materials

Base coat - White low-sheen acrylic enamel

Glaze #1 - 1 part green and 2 parts water

Glaze #2 - 1 part sienna and 2 parts water
(Artists' acrylic paint may be substituted
due to the small amount required.)

Glaze #3 - 1 part black and 1 part water
(Artists' acrylic paint may again be
substituted).

Glaze #4 - 1 part light green and 1 part
glazing liquid

Acrylic varnish

Tools

Natural wool sea sponge

Medium round artists' brush

Note: Because the glazes used in this pattern are highly diluted, they're suitable only
for applying to horizontal surfaces.

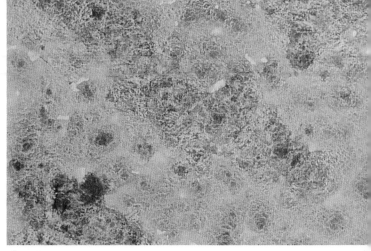

1. After applying the base color to the project surface, allow the surface to dry.

2. Wash the natural sea sponge under running water to free it of loose ocean particles, and squeeze out the excess water. Then use the sponge to apply glaze #1 to the project surface. Dab the glaze onto the surface to create a mottled, uneven pattern (see plate 84). Clean the sponge, and let the project surface dry thoroughly.

3. Use the medium round-tipped artists' brush to apply the sienna glaze (glaze #2) to the green background created in the previous step. Weave the veining throughout the darker-valued areas left by the sponge, and let the veins meander and vary in width (plate 85). Wash the artists' brush, and let the surface dry.

4. Using the artists' brush, apply the black glaze (glaze #3) to echo the vein patterns established in step 3 (plate 86). Allow the surface to dry.

5. Moisten the natural sea sponge, and use it to apply glaze #4 to the project surface. The purpose of this glaze is to set the veins within the surface of the sample so that they appear to exist within the marble, not just on top of it. Dab the glaze onto the surface, covering the vein patterns partially, but not completely. If the project surface is large, use the vein pattern to establish breaks; work up to the vein on one side, and continue on the other side after a break. This will help to avoid lap marks in the surface.

6. When the surface is dry, apply the acrylic varnish. Heavily diluted paint isn't durable and requires this additional protection.

Plate 84

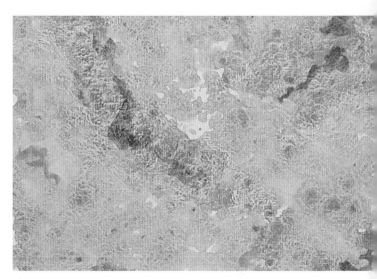

Plate 85

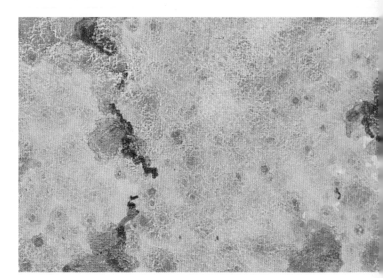

Plate 86

Stylized Malachite

BASE COAT
White low-sheen
acrylic enamel

GLAZE
1 part green, 1 part water,
and 1 part glazing liquid

Plate 87

Materials

Base coat - White low-sheen acrylic enamel

Glaze - 1 part green, 1 part water, and 1 part
    glazing liquid

Acrylic varnish

Tools

Sumi blending brush

1. Apply the base color to the project surface,
   and let it dry.

2. Load a liberal amount of glaze onto the
   sumi blending brush. Then jiggle the
   brush while moving it in meandering "S"
   and "C" patterns across the surface of your
   project. Stop-and-go lap marks look unnat-
   ural in this pattern, so avoid these marks
   by crossing them with fresh glaze while
   they're still wet. Clean the brush, and
   allow the surface to dry.

3. Apply an acrylic varnish.

Pearl Gray

Materials

Base coat - White low-sheen acrylic enamel

Glaze #1 - 1 part navy blue and 2 parts water

Glaze #2 - 1 part steel blue and 2 parts water

Glaze #3 - 1 part white and 1 part glazing liquid

Acrylic varnish

Tools

Natural wool sea sponge

Note: Because the glazes used in this pattern are highly diluted, they're suitable only for applying to horizontal surfaces.

1. Apply the base color to the project surface, and allow it to dry.

2. Apply glaze #1 to your project surface with the natural sea sponge. Dab the glaze onto the surface; the glaze should sit on the surface in small, random blots created by the pores in the sponge. When the surface is covered, allow it to dry. Then wash and rinse the sponge.

3. Blot glaze #2 onto the surface, leaving traces of the previous glaze uncovered to create the effect of wide, free-flowing veins. Allow the surface to dry, and wash and rinse the sponge.

4. Apply glaze #3 to the surface in the same manner that glaze #2 was applied. Now blot the surface everywhere except where you created veins in the previous step. This glaze deepens the veined effect and lightens the overall surface. When you're satisfied with the results, allow the surface to dry.

5. Apply an acrylic varnish.

BASE COAT
White low-sheen
acrylic enamel

GLAZE #1
1 part navy blue and
2 parts water

GLAZE #2
1 part steel blue and
2 parts water

GLAZE #3
1 part white and
1 part glazing liquid

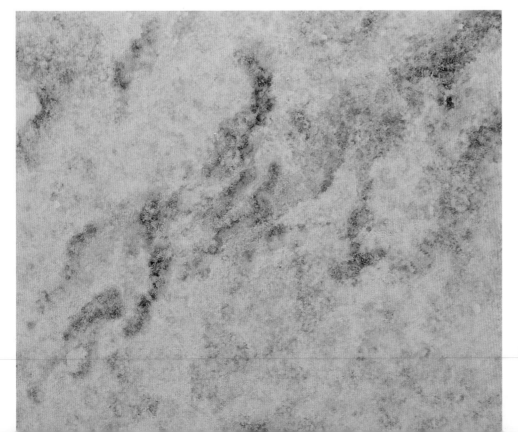

Plate 88

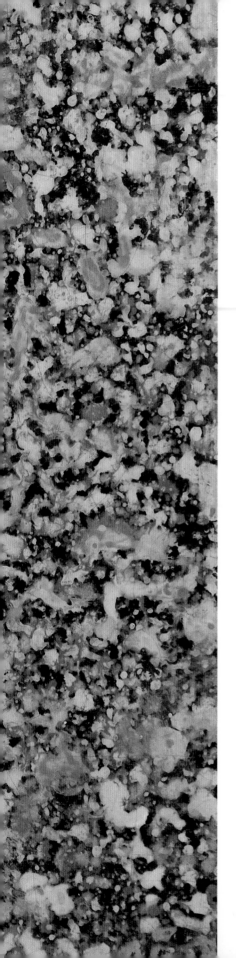

Granite

G RANITE FINISHES ARE PRODUCED MOST FREQUENTLY ON COLUMNS, MANTELS, TABLETOPS, FLOORS, AND OTHER SUR-FACES THAT ARE TRADITIONALLY MADE OF STONE. THE LAY-ERED FLECKS OF MULTIPLE COLORS IN A SIMULATED GRANITE SAMPLE GIVE THE ILLUSION OF WEIGHT AND DENSITY, REGARDLESS OF THE COLOR COMBINATION. IT'S EASY TO OBTAIN THE EFFECT OF GRANITE IN THE COLORS THAT YOU WANT TO USE. THE PLATES IN THIS CHAPTER INCLUDE REPRO-DUCTIONS OF ACTUAL TYPES OF GRANITE AND SOME SAMPLES THAT ARE PURE FANTASY.

Pink Himilaia

Plate 89

BASE COAT
Warm umber low-sheen
acrylic enamel

GLAZE #1
1 part black, 1 part water,
and 1 part glazing liquid

GLAZE #2
1 part salmon, 1 part water,
and 1 part glazing liquid

GLAZE #3
1 part ochre, 1 part water,
and 1 part glazing liquid

GLAZE #4
1 part beige, 1 part water,
and 1 part glazing liquid

Materials

Base coat - Warm umber low-sheen
   acrylic enamel

Glaze #1 - 1 part black, 1 part water, and 1
   part glazing liquid

Glaze #2 - 1 part salmon, 1 part water, and 1
   part glazing liquid

Glaze #3 - 1 part ochre, 1 part water, and 1
   part glazing liquid

Glaze #4 - 1 part beige, 1 part water, and 1
   part glazing liquid

Acrylic varnish

Tools

Cultured sea sponge

Clean cotton rags

Shallow pan

Pink Himilaia

1. Apply the base color to the project surface, and let it dry.

2. To remove loose ocean particles, clean the cultured sea sponge under running water. Squeeze out the excess moisture; then dip the sponge into the black glaze (glaze #1). Lightly dab any excess glaze onto a clean rag, and use the sponge to blot the glaze onto the project surface. To create an even stippled surface, use a perpendicular dabbing motion to apply the glaze (see plate 90). Clean the sponge, and allow the surface to dry.

3. Use the same technique to apply the salmon-colored glaze (glaze #2), but load the sponge with somewhat more glaze, and apply slightly more pressure when dabbing the project surface. This extra pigment will ensure that the salmon pink is the dominant color in this pattern (plate 91). Clean the sponge, and let the surface dry.

4. Use the technique described in step 2 to apply the ochre glaze (glaze #3, see plate 92). Clean the sponge, and allow the surface to dry.

5. Using the same method, apply the beige glaze (glaze #4).

6. When the surface is dry, apply an acrylic varnish.

Plate 90

Plate 91

Plate 92

Blanco Castelo

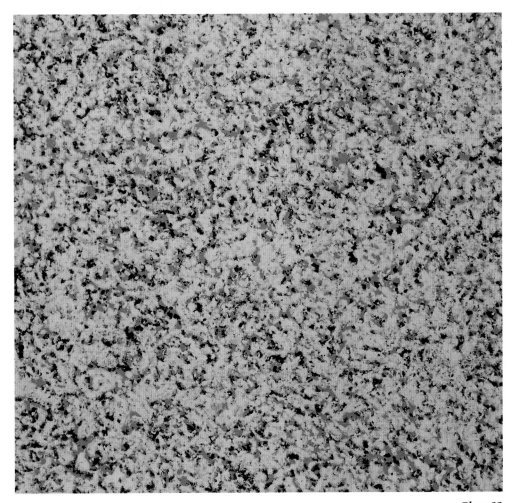

BASE COAT
Warm umber-gray low-sheen acrylic enamel

GLAZE #1
Undiluted
black acrylic enamel

GLAZE #2
1 part gray, 1 part water,
and 1 part glazing liquid

Plate 93

Materials

Base coat - Warm umber-gray low-sheen
   acrylic enamel

Glaze #1 - Undiluted black acrylic enamel

Glaze #2 - 1 part gray, 1 part water, and 1
   part glazing liquid

Acrylic varnish

Tools

Cultured sea sponge

Natural wool sea sponge

Clean cotton rags

Refer to the instructions for Pink Himilaia for
the basic procedure; this pattern uses two
types of sponges to alter the scale and clarity
of the granite texture. Use the cultured
sponge to apply the undiluted black paint to
the surface, and the wool sponge to apply
the gray glaze.

Tolga

BASE COAT
Warm umber-gray low
sheen acrylic enamel

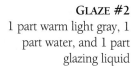

GLAZE #1
Undiluted black
acrylic enamel

GLAZE #2
1 part warm light gray, 1
part water, and 1 part
glazing liquid

Plate 94

Materials

Base coat - Warm umber-gray low-sheen
acrylic enamel

Glaze #1 - Undiluted black acrylic enamel

Glaze #2 - 1 part warm light gray, 1 part
water, and 1 part glazing liquid

Acrylic varnish

Tools

Cultured sea sponge

Natural wool sponge

Clean cotton rags

This pattern requires the same colors as those
used in the previous sample (Blanco Castelo),
but the final glaze is applied twice. The resulting surface is subtler and more uniform. Refer
to Pink Himilaia and Blanco Castelo for general instructions.

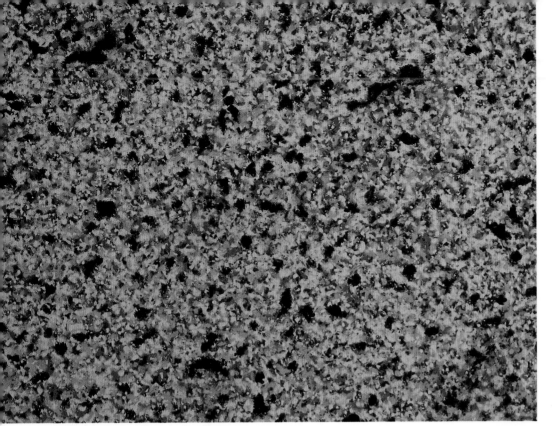

Silver Sea Green

Plate 95

Materials

Base coat - Black low-sheen acrylic enamel

Glaze #1 - 1 part dark gray-green, 1 part water, and 1 part glazing liquid

Glaze #2 - 1 part medium gray, 1 part water, and 1 part glazing liquid

Glaze #3 - 1 part rusty orange, 1 part water, and 1 part glazing liquid

Glaze #4 - 1 part olive green, 1 part water, and 1 part glazing liquid

Glaze #5 - 1 part light olive green, 1 part water, and 1 part glazing liquid

Acrylic varnish

Tools

Natural wool sponge

Natural grass sponge

Clean cotton rags

Small round-tipped artists' brush

Follow the basic instructions for Pink Himilaia, applying glazes #1 and #2 with the wool sponge, and glazes #3, #4, and #5 with the grass sponge. Then use the small round-tipped artists' brush to add black flecks to the project surface. These flecks should vary in size and should take advantage of the organic shapes that have developed on the surface. Notice that although these flecks are opaque and contrast sharply with the painted background, they recede into the surface visually. This is due to the black base coat, which, although it was almost entirely obscured by subsequent glazes, provides a visual connection to the black flecks. Allow the surface to dry; then apply an acrylic varnish.

BASE COAT
Black low-sheen
acrylic enamel

GLAZE #1
1 part dark gray-green,
1 part water, and
1 part glazing liquid

GLAZE #2
1 part medium gray,
1 part water, and
1 part glazing liquid

GLAZE #3
1 part rusty orange,
1 part water, and
1 part glazing liquid

GLAZE #4
1 part olive green,
1 part water, and
1 part glazing liquid

GLAZE #5
1 part light olive green,
1 part water, and
1 part glazing liquid

Pink Salisbury

BASE COAT
White low-sheen
acrylic enamel

GLAZE #1
1 part medium brown
and 2 parts water

GLAZE #2
1 part coral
and 2 parts water

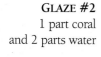

GLAZE #3
1 part dark brown
and 1 part water

GLAZE #4
1 part light coral and
2 parts water

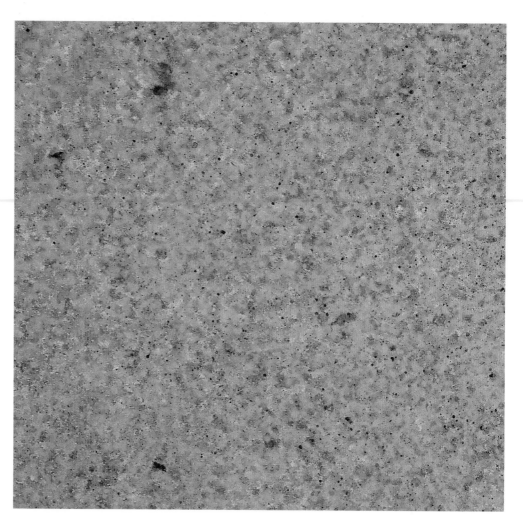

Plate 96

Materials

Base coat - White low-sheen acrylic enamel

Glaze #1 - 1 part medium brown and
2 parts water

Glaze #2 - 1 part coral and 2 parts water

Glaze #3 - 1 part dark brown and
1 part water

Glaze #4 - 1 part light coral and
2 parts water

Acrylic varnish

Tools

Natural wool sea sponge

Medium stiff-bristled artists' brush

Shallow pan

Note: Because the glazes used in this pattern are highly diluted, they're suitable only for applying to horizontal surfaces.

1. Apply the base color to the project surface.

2. After rinsing the sea sponge under running water to free it of loose ocean particles, squeeze out the excess moisture. Pour the brown glaze (glaze #1) into the shallow pan, and dip the sponge into it. Dab the glaze onto the project surface to create a flecked, contrasting pattern. In order to achieve an organic, pooled texture, the thin glaze must be applied liberally with a soggy sponge. The resulting surface should be very wet (see plate 97). Once the surface is completely covered, rinse out the sponge and shallow pan. Be sure to allow the surface to dry before proceeding to step 3.

3. Apply the coral-colored glaze (glaze #2) using the technique described above (plate 98). Then, while the project surface dries, clean the sponge and shallow pan.

4. With the stiff-bristled artists' brush, apply blots of dark brown glaze (glaze #3) randomly to the surface. Use the same glaze to spatter tiny flecks onto the surface (plate 99). In one hand, hold the brush so that the bristles are parallel to the surface. Using the index finger of your other hand, pull back the bristles, and release them to spatter the project surface. Repeat this motion until the area is evenly covered. Then allow the surface to dry.

5. Using the technique described in step 2, apply the light coral glaze (glaze #4) to the surface, and let it dry.

6. Apply an acrylic varnish to the completed project.

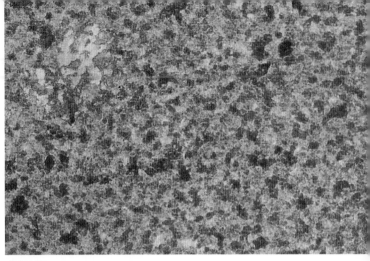

Plate 97

Plate 98

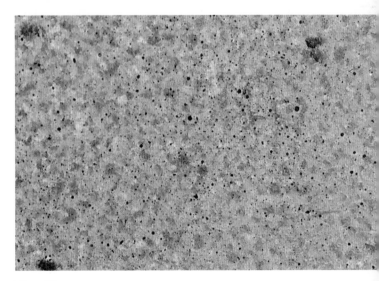

Plate 99

Luna Pearl

BASE COAT
Warm dark gray
low-sheen acrylic enamel

GLAZE #1
4 parts black and
1 part water

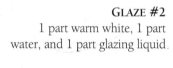

GLAZE #2
1 part warm white, 1 part
water, and 1 part glazing liquid.

GLAZE #3
1 part pink, 1 part water,
and 1 part glazing liquid

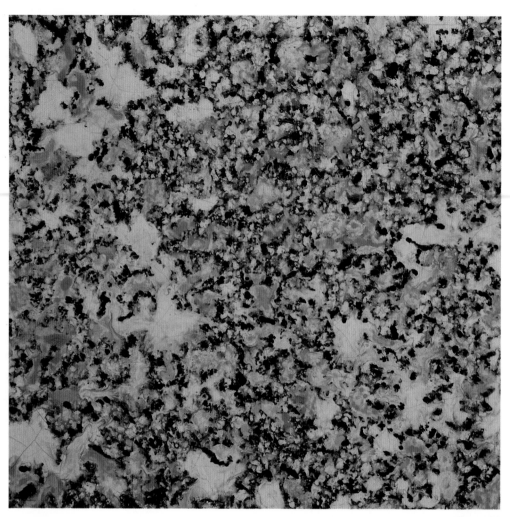

Plate 100

Materials

Base coat - Warm dark gray low-sheen
acrylic enamel

Glaze #1 - 4 parts black and 1 part water

Glaze #2 - 1 part warm white, 1 part water,
and 1 part glazing liquid

Glaze #3 - 1 part pink, 1 part water, and 1
part glazing liquid

Acrylic varnish

Tools

Natural wool sea sponge

Shallow pan

Medium round-tipped artists' brush

Clean cotton rags

1. Apply the base color to the project surface, and let it dry.

2. After cleaning and wringing out the wool sponge, pour the black glaze (glaze #1) into the shallow pan. Dip the sponge into the pan, and lightly blot any excess glaze onto a clean rag. To create a definite spotted texture, apply the glaze using a dabbing motion that is perpendicular to your project surface. As you create the texture, try to leave about 50 percent of the base color uncovered (see plate 101). Rinse out the sponge and pan, and let the surface dry.

3. Using the method described above, apply the white glaze (glaze #2) to the surface (plate 102). Allow the surface to dry.

4. With the medium round artists' brush, apply the pink glaze (glaze #3) over portions of the white glaze laid down in the previous step. This color should be added sparingly, so dab the excess glaze onto a rag, if necessary, before applying it. Rinse out the brush, and let the surface dry.

5. Use the artists' brush to reapply the warm white glaze (glaze #2) to the white areas laid down in step 3. Your goal is to create large, organic blots. Again, rid the brush of excess glaze if necessary.

6. When the project surface is dry, apply an acrylic varnish.

Plate 101

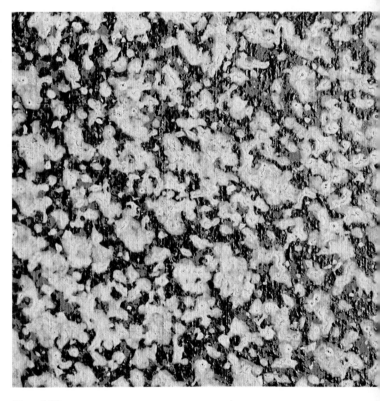

Plate 102

Splattered Granite

BASE COAT
White low-sheen
acrylic enamel

GLAZE #1
1 part black, 1 part water,
and 1 part glazing liquid

GLAZE #2
1 part medium brown, 1 part
water, and 1 part glazing liquid

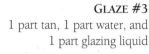

GLAZE #3
1 part tan, 1 part water, and
1 part glazing liquid

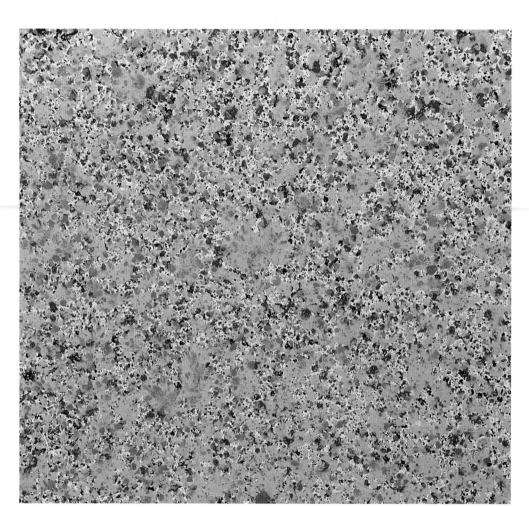

Plate 103

Materials

Base coat - White low-sheen acrylic enamel

Glaze #1 - 1 part black, 1 part water, and 1 part glazing liquid

Glaze #2 - 1 part medium brown, 1 part water, and 1 part glazing liquid

Glaze #3 - 1 part tan, 1 part water, and 1 part glazing liquid

Acrylic varnish

Tools

Synthetic bristle brush

Wooden block (see step 2)

1. Apply the base color to the project, and let it dry.

2. There are two methods for achieving a splattered granite finish. In the first, you tap the loaded brush against a stationary object (such as a wooden block) held in your other hand (see figure 10). The second method is a bit faster but messier: you manually bend back the bristles of the brush with one hand while pushing the brush forward with the other (figure 11). Regardless of the method used, rubber gloves are advised. If the latter method is selected, use an old brush since the repeated manipulation of the bristles can damage the brush.

   Once you have chosen a method of application, use it to splatter the black glaze onto the project surface, covering the surface as uniformly as possible. Clean out the brush, and allow the surface to dry.

3. Following the same procedure that you used for glaze #1, apply glaze #2. Then wash the brush, and let the surface dry.

4. Use the same technique to apply glaze #3.

5. When the surface is dry, apply an acrylic varnish.

Figure 10

Figure 11

Wood Graining

WOOD GRAINING—THE PAINTED REPLICATION OF WOOD'S SURFACE—WAS ONCE A COMMON PRACTICE; IT ALLOWED A CRAFTSPERSON TO IMITATE COSTLY HARDWOODS ON FURNITURE OR MILLWORK MADE FROM INEXPENSIVE SOFTWOODS OR METAL. THIS CRAFT IS CURRENTLY ENJOYING A RESURGENCE IN POPULARITY. IT'S MORE COST-EFFECTIVE, FOR EXAMPLE, TO APPLY A GRAINED FINISH TO OLD, PAINTED WOOD THAN IT IS TO STRIP AND REFINISH IT. ALSO, NEW BUILDING MATERIALS MADE OF PLASTICS AND WOOD COMPOSITES (STYROFOAM OR FIBERBOARD, FOR EXAMPLE) CAN BE FINISHED TO RESEMBLE EXPENSIVE HARDWOODS. FINALLY, WOOD GRAINING IS ENVIRONMENTALLY SENSIBLE; IT OFFERS THE APPEARANCE OF RARE WOODS WITHOUT THE NEED TO PARTICIPATE IN THE WORLD'S DEFORESTATION.

THIS CHAPTER INCLUDES SEVEN SAMPLES WITH A RANGE OF COLORS, TEXTURES, AND GRAIN PATTERNS. THESE ARE PRIMARILY TROPICAL HARDWOODS, PRIZED FOR THEIR DISTINCTIVE PATTERNING AND RARITY. ALSO INCLUDED ARE A FEW SAMPLES OF MORE COMMON FURNITURE-GRADE HARDWOODS SUCH AS OAK AND WALNUT. THESE SAMPLES REPRESENT THE COLOR OF NEWLY CUT WOOD. SINCE SOME WOODS DARKEN OVER TIME, IT MAY BE NECESSARY TO USE A DARKER BASE COAT IF AN OLD WOOD APPEARANCE IS DESIRED.

Plate 104. It is not necessary to strip layers of old paint in order to achieve the appearance of fine woodwork. The doors and moldings in this study were grained with a dark mahogany finish. The method used to create this effect appears on page 104–5.

Graining Tools

Plate 105. Left to right, *graining rocker, oak grain roller, and graining combs.*

Graining tools—combs and rockers—are subtractive. They remove or alter a wet layer of glaze to simulate the patterns of wood grain. Since the glaze must be manipulated while it's still wet, you should work just one band of glaze at a time. For large areas, it's helpful to subdivide the area into individual "boards" and to work on every other board. When the first series has dried, remove the masking tape, and grain the remaining boards. This allows you to work on small areas and to maintain a wet surface. To soften the grain patterns created by these tools, wisp over the painted surface with a dry sumi brush.

Graining tools are limited in their application; because of their flat, rigid construction, they work well only on flat surfaces such as walls and tabletops. The samples shown in plates 106 through 111 illustrate the effects that you can produce using graining tools. The rest of the samples in this chapter were created using inexpensive painting tools; these tools, which are additive, can be used for flat areas as well as more complicated surfaces such as cove moldings and beveled trim work.

GRAINING COMBS

Graining combs are used to replicate quarter-sawn or vertical-grain wood such as fir. These combs are ordinarily sold at paint stores, and they come in a pack containing several sizes. The size of each comb is determined by its width and the spacing of its teeth. As these samples illustrate (plates 106, 107, and 108), graining combs can be used to create a variety of grain patterns.

When using a graining comb, your base coat should be a low-sheen acrylic enamel, opaquely applied, and your glaze should be one part paint, one part water, and one part glazing liquid.

The first sample (plate 106) illustrates the simplest graining technique using a comb. Apply the base coat, and let it dry. Then, with a synthetic bristle brush, apply the glaze evenly and vertically. Drag the graining comb through the glaze to create a stylized vertical grain pattern, and use a rag to wipe excess glaze from the comb.

To replicate the second example (plate 107), start by repeating the steps from the first example. Then create the rippling marks by holding the comb at a slight angle and dragging it over the vertical grain pattern. Repeat these angled strokes to achieve the ribbon patterns seen in the photograph.

The third sample (plate 108) is subtler than the previous two; it's achieved by wrapping the teeth of the comb with cheesecloth prior to dragging it through the glaze. Wrap the cloth at least twice around the comb—or more times if a more delicate texture is desired.

GRAINING ROCKERS

Graining rockers are useful tools that simulate the grain of flat-sawn wood. They can be used to create a wide array of effects, and you should exploit this flexibility when replicating wood grain. Real wood grain varies a great deal in width and pattern across a single board, and a graining rocker allows you to create a similar range of patterns on your projects.

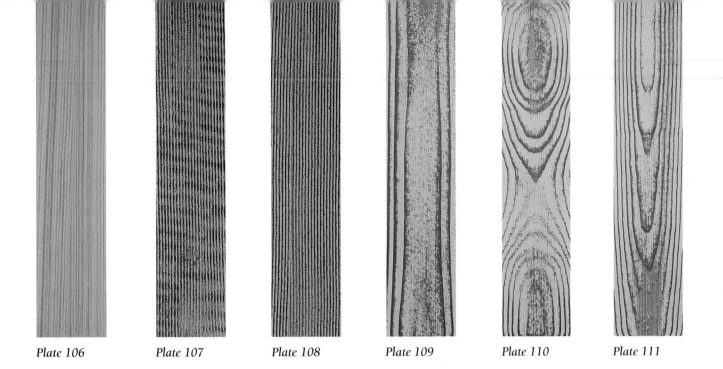

Plate 106   Plate 107   Plate 108   Plate 109   Plate 110   Plate 111

Graining rockers are available in many different sizes, but regardless of size, their construction is basically the same. A rocker's working surface is either cylindrical, or semicylindrical, with a series of raised concentric rings on its rubber surface. This rubber pad is attached to a handle that is used to drag and rock the tool over wet paint to produce a wood-grain pattern. Due to the round shape of the tool, its use is limited to flat surfaces without raised edges.

General instructions for using a graining rocker call for a base coat that is a low-sheen acrylic enamel, opaquely applied, and a glaze that is one part acrylic enamel, one part water, and one part glazing liquid. Apply the base coat, and let it dry. Then apply the glaze with a synthetic bristle brush, brushing it on parallel to the intended grain direction. While the glaze is wet, drag the graining rocker through it.

In the example shown in plate 109, the tool is dragged through the glaze with a minimum of rocking motion. In the second sample (plate 110), the tool is rocked slowly as it is dragged, resulting in an elongated grain pattern.

Plate 111 shows the results gained when the tool is rocked vigorously back and forth as it's dragged through the glaze. When dragging and rocking the tool through the glaze, keep both movements smooth and steady, and apply constant and even pressure. Don't stop midway across the surface; each simulated board should be grained with one continuous motion (see figure 12).

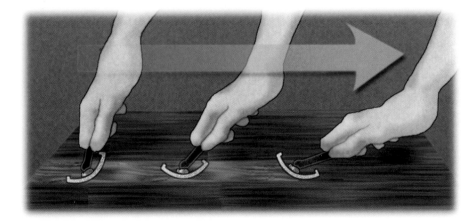

Figure 12

Mahogany

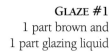

BASE COAT
Deep red to deep orange
low-sheen acrylic enamel

GLAZE #1
1 part brown and
1 part glazing liquid

Plate 112

To achieve the subtle ribbon pattern that is characteristic of mahogany, a lot of blending is required. In order to develop a good working rhythm, practice on scrap material before starting on the project surface.

Materials

Base coat - Deep red to deep orange low-sheen acrylic enamel

Glaze - 1 part brown and 1 part glazing liquid

Acrylic varnish

Tools

Sumi blending brush

Two tapered blending brushes

Cotton rags

1. Apply the base color to your project surface. Opaque coverage is required, so apply two to three coats. Then allow the base color to dry.

2. Use a tapered blending brush to apply vertical bands of glaze to the project surface, applying two bands at a time (see plate 113). Then proceed to the next step.

3. As soon as the glaze is laid down in step 2, it should be blended. Using a dry sumi blending brush, gently wisp the glaze first against (plate 114), then with (plate 115) the direction of the bands applied in step 2. The goal is to create a noticeably ribboned pattern that varies in color from the original base coat to the dark brown glaze. When the blending brush picks up too much glaze, wipe it off on a rag.

4. To simulate the open pores typical of mahogany, use a dry tapered blending brush. Create the pore marks by holding the brush at an angle of about 30 degrees to the project surface and pouncing the tips of the bristles into the wet glaze. When the strip is finished, return to step 2. If there are stray glaze marks on the edge of the current strip, wipe them off with a wet rag prior to creating the next band. Because mahogany is so straight grained, it should be easy to make the transition from one band to the next.

5. When the entire project surface is dry, apply an acrylic varnish.

Plate 113

Plate 114

Plate 115

Zebrawood

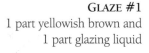

BASE COAT
Deep ochre, low-sheen
acrylic enamel

GLAZE #1
1 part yellowish brown and
1 part glazing liquid

GLAZE #2
1 part medium brown and
1 part glazing liquid

GLAZE #3
1 part dark chocolate brown
and 1 part glazing liquid

Plate 116

Zebrawood is an African hardwood that, when sawn, displays a bold, vertical striped grain that alternates between yellow ochre and dark chocolate brown. This distinctive striping gives zebrawood its name and provides an interesting design option.

Materials

Base coat - Deep ochre, low-sheen
    acrylic enamel

Glaze #1 - 1 part yellowish brown and 1 part
    glazing liquid

Glaze #2 - 1 part medium brown and 1 part
    glazing liquid

Glaze #3 - 1 part dark chocolate brown and
    1 part glazing liquid

Acrylic varnish

Tools

1-1/2" (3.8 cm) synthetic bristle brush

Modified 4" (10.2-cm) foam brush
    (see figure 13)

Two sumi blending brushes

Small blunt artists' brush

Cotton rags

Cotton swabs

Plate 117

Plate 118

Plate 119

Plate 120

1. Apply two or three coats of the base color to the project surface, making sure you have opaque coverage. Allow the surface to dry.

2. With the flat synthetic brush, apply glaze #1 to the project surface. Create stripes the width of the brush, leaving 3/4-inch (1.9-cm) gaps between stripes (see plate 117). Allow the surface to dry, and clean your brush for use in step 3.

3. Using the synthetic brush, apply glaze #2 to the surface, centering your brush on the spaces between the stripes created in step 2 (plate 118). Allow the glaze to dry.

4. Apply glaze #3 to the surface using the notched foam brush to create distinct vertical grain lines. To prevent uneven glaze coverage, dab the brush on an absorbent rag prior to application. In order to create continuous vertical grain patterns, it's necessary to align and overlap brush strokes after reloading the brush. These overlapping strokes will look dark and obvious (plate 119). To obscure them, wisp over these areas with a dry brush before the glaze dries; then use a damp cotton swab to remove the resulting smudge marks from the background colors. Allow the glaze to dry.

5. To simulate the open pores seen in natural wood, dip the dry blending brush into the brown glaze (glaze #3) so that only the very tips of the bristles are covered. Lightly stipple the project surface. While these marks are wet, soften them by sweeping them lightly with the other dry blending brush (plate 120). Allow the surface to dry.

6. The knots in zebrawood are small and fairly inconspicuous, but they add variety and interest to the dominating striped pattern, and they're easy to replicate. Using a small round artists' brush, simply paint a small teardrop shape between two grain lines (with glaze #3). Dab the excess glaze from your brush onto a rag; then place the tip of the brush into the center of the teardrop, and twist it to create the knot. Allow the knots to dry, and apply an acrylic clear coat over the project surface.

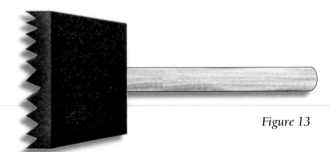

Figure 13

Ebony

BASE COAT
Stock black low sheen acrylic enamel modified with red oxide.

GLAZE #1
4 parts very dark chocolate brown and 1 part water

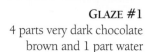

GLAZE #2
4 parts sienna and 1 part water

Plate 121

Ebony is prized for its rich black hue and extremely dense grain. It's used mostly as a decorative wood and is so expensive that it's sold by the ounce rather than the board foot. Fortunately, ebony is also an easy wood to replicate.

Materials

Base coat - Use a "stock black" low sheen acrylic enamel. Since this is a cool black, have the paint store add 1 ounce (29.6 ml) of red oxide per quart (.9 l) of stock black.

Glaze #1 - 4 parts very dark chocolate brown and 1 part water

Glaze #2 - 4 parts sienna and 1 part water

Acrylic clear finish

Tools

Flat synthetic bristle brush

Tapered natural bristle brush

Thin artists' brush

Sumi blending brush

Cotton rags

1. Using the synthetic bristle brush, apply the base coat to the project surface. Stock black has excellent hiding capacity, so one coat should provide opaque coverage. Allow the surface to dry.

2. Dip the tapered brush about halfway up the bristles into glaze #1. After lightly blotting the excess glaze onto a clean rag, wisp a straight grain pattern onto the black base coat (see plate 122). When the pattern is complete, let the glaze dry for at least an hour, and clean your brush for use in step 3.

Plate 122

3. Apply the sienna glaze (glaze #2) to the project surface as you applied glaze #1 in the previous step, but use less glaze on the brush. Your goal is to create thin, hairline graining to accent the brushwork already accomplished (plate 123). Allow the glaze to dry.

4. Create a bolder sienna grain by applying glaze #2 with a thin artists' brush and a sumi blending brush. Use the artists' brush to make thin, wavering vertical marks; then—before the glaze dries—gently wisp over these marks first against, then with the grain. Work on only a few streaks at a time because the glaze must remain wet for proper blending. Once the glaze has dried, highlight these grain marks by reapplying the glaze over portions of the blended strokes. Then soften them immediately with the blending brush (plate 124).

Plate 123

5. When the project surface is entirely dry, apply a clear coat of acrylic varnish.

Plate 124

Paduak

Plate 125

Paduak is an African hardwood noted for its deep red hue and vertical banding, which typically varies from 1/4 to 1/2 inch (.6 to 1.3 cm) in width. Replication of paduak requires a lot of blending, and while these instructions are set up for solo work, it's helpful to have an assistant.

Materials

Base coat - Reddish orange low-sheen acrylic enamel, dark in value

Glaze #1 - 1 part dark rust and 1 part glazing liquid

Glaze #2 - 2 parts brown and 1 part glazing liquid

Acrylic varnish

Tools

Modified graining brush (see figure 14)

Two dry blending brushes

Medium round artists' brush

Cotton rags

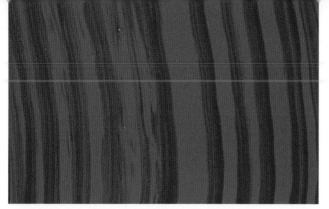

Plate 126

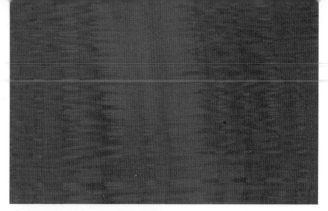

Plate 127

Plate 128

Plate 129

1. When applying the base color to the project surface, expect to use two to three coats to obtain the opaque coverage required. After it is totally covered, allow the surface to dry.

2. Dip the graining brush into glaze #1, and blot the excess paint onto a rag. Then brush the glaze onto the project surface in a subtle "S" pattern, working in small areas so that your brush strokes remain wet for blending (see plate 126).

3. Using the first dry blending brush, gently brush against (plate 127), then with (plate 128) the grain. Variations in color should appear as soft, flowing stripes. Continue the process, alternating steps 2 and 3, until the entire project surface is covered. Let the glaze dry completely.

4. Using the artists' brush, apply more of glaze #1 to enhance the grain ribbons created in the previous steps. Keep the brush strokes evident (do not blend), but don't make them so thick that they obscure the underlying grain pattern (plate 129). Allow the glaze to dry.

5. This step replicates the open pores that are typical of paduak. Dip a blending brush into the brown glaze (glaze #2) so that only the very tips of the bristles are covered. Holding the brush perpendicular to the project surface, dab it lightly to produce a stippled pattern. Before these flecks dry, wisp them gently parallel to the grain with the second dry blending brush. Work in small areas to allow blending.

6. After the surface dries, apply a coat of acrylic varnish.

Figure 14

Wenge

BASE COAT
Low-sheen acrylic enamel

GLAZE #1
1 part black and
1 part glazing liquid

GLAZE #2
Untinted glazing liquid

Plate 130

Wenge is a decorative hardwood characterized by its tight, figured grain. This wood is best replicated using a black water-soluble crayon, which can be purchased at art supply stores. (Hydromarker is one brand name.) The crayon remains soluble after it has been applied to the surface, making it easy to blend.

Materials

Base coat - Low-sheen acrylic enamel—the base color can range from brick orange to dark chocolate brown. Brick orange yields better results because it makes a more dramatic contrast with the tight, black grain pattern.

Glaze #1 - 1 part black and 1 part glazing liquid

Glaze # 2 - Untinted glazing liquid

Acrylic varnish

Tools

Tapered natural bristle brush

Sumi blending brush

Black water-soluble crayon

Straightedge

Cotton rags

1. Apply the base coat to the project surface. Because a black glaze is overlaid later, opaque coverage of the base coat isn't critical. Allow it to dry completely.

2. This sample utilizes two types of grain patterns: the streaked, fairly uniform vertical grain pattern, and the arched, freehand flat grain pattern. With the water-soluble crayon and the straightedge, establish two parallel, vertical lines on the project surface. These lines represent the outer edges of the flat-grained section of your sample, and they can be as far apart as is proportionate to the project. On the outer sides of the guide lines, create a vertical grain pattern using the tapered brush and the black glaze (glaze #1). Load the brush so that it carries enough glaze to cover the entire length of the project surface in one stroke, but don't overload it, or the base coat will be obscured (see plate 131). Allow at least one hour for the surface to dry.

3. Now use the water-soluble crayon to draw the flat-grain pattern. The grain bands should be close together and thin near the vertical grain sections, and they should broaden and expand to the center of this section (plate 132).

4. Dip the blending brush into the transparent glazing liquid (glaze #2), and blot the excess glaze onto a rag. Lightly brush this solution over the central band. This process softens the crayon marks and binds the crayon into the glazing liquid, making it permanent (plate 133). Let the glaze dry thoroughly.

5. With the tapered brush, wisp on a light coating of the black glaze (glaze #1) over the entire project surface. This darkens the overall appearance and unifies the different grain patterns.

6. After allowing the project surface to dry, apply an acrylic varnish.

Plate 131

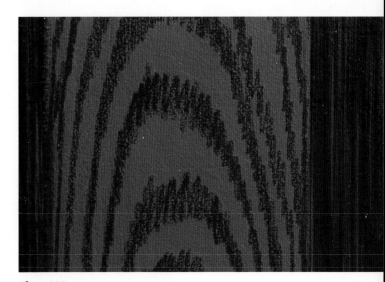

Plate 132

Plate 133

Walnut Burl

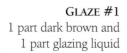

BASE COAT
Brown low-sheen
acrylic enamel

GLAZE #1
1 part dark brown and
1 part glazing liquid

GLAZE #2
1 part dark brown, 1 part water,
and 1 part glazing liquid

Plate 134

Burled woods are organic, unpredictable, and very detailed. At first glance, they look impossible to replicate. However, by using a succession of thin glaze coats, they're actually quite easy to master.

Materials

Base coat - Brown low-sheen acrylic enamel

Glaze #1 -1 part dark brown and 1 part glazing liquid

Glaze #2 - 1 part dark brown, 1 part water, and 1 part glazing liquid

Acrylic varnish

Tools

Medium round-tipped artists' brush

Large round-tipped artists' brush (preferably one with long bristles)

Sumi blending brush

Shallow pan

Cotton rags

1. Apply two coats of the base color. An opaque base coat isn't critical because subsequent layers of dark glaze will hide most of the underlying base color.

2. Dip the tip of the medium artists' brush into the first glaze. Then, holding the brush perpendicular to the painted surface, press down and twist to form small clusters of little swirls (see plate 135). Allow these to dry for at least one hour.

3. Using the large artists' brush, test glaze #2 on a small area of the painted surface. If it lacks transparency, dilute it with more water. Then apply the glaze in a swirling, organic motion, allowing the bristles to leave fine grain lines (plate 136). Allow at least one hour for drying, and retain this glaze mixture for use in the following step.

4. When the painted surface is completely dry, repeat the previous step, but load more glaze onto the brush. Press down on the brush while twisting and moving it in random patterns. Work in small enough areas to allow the glaze to remain wet for blending (plate 137). The secret to replicating burl woods is to layer different techniques; each layer covers the previous step but doesn't totally obscure it.

5. Using short, gentle, sweeping strokes in all directions with the dry blending brush, blend the glaze coat that was just applied.

6. Once the glaze is dry, apply an acrylic clear finish.

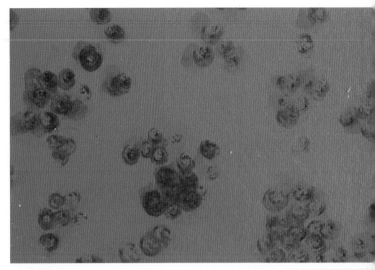

Plate 135

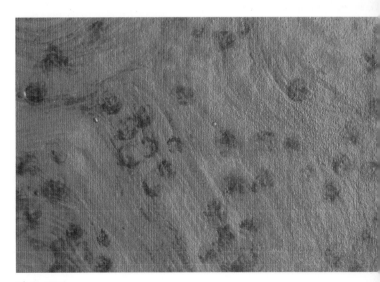

Plate 136

Plate 137

Oak

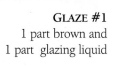

BASE COAT
Deep ochre low-sheen
acrylic enamel

GLAZE #1
1 part brown and
1 part glazing liquid

GLAZE #2
1 part sienna, and
1 part glazing liquid

Plate 138

Oak is probably the most common hardwood available in North America. It's used for flooring, cabinetwork, furniture, and trim. Most of the oak sold is flat-sawn, which is the most efficient way to turn a log into lumber. The sample shown here, however, is quartersawn oak. This cut is less efficient—and therefore more expensive—to produce. Quartersawn oak was a common choice for Arts and Crafts and Mission furniture.

Materials

Base coat - Deep ochre low-sheen
    acrylic enamel

Glaze #1 - 1 part brown and 1 part
    glazing liquid

Glaze #2 - 1 part sienna and 1 part
    glazing liquid

Acrylic varnish

Tools

Medium round-tipped artists' brush

Tapered natural bristle brush

Cotton rags

Cotton swabs

Oak grain roller

Shallow pan

Although this book is geared toward the use of common, inexpensive tools, this wood pattern calls for a specialty tool. An oak grain roller looks similar to a pasta cutter, but each wheel has cuts varying in size and interval. This tool will help you to replicate the short, unwavering pores that are characteristic of oak.

1. Apply two to three coats of the deep ochre base coat. To achieve good results, it's important that this surface be opaque. Once complete coverage has been obtained, allow the surface to dry.

2. Pour a shallow, wide bead of glaze #1 into the pan. Wet the grain roller by rolling it through the bead of glaze. Make sure that the entire circumference of the roller is wet. Then roll the grain onto the base coat, overlapping strokes to achieve an even distribution of pattern (see plate 139). Cover only enough area to maintain a wet surface for step 3, and retain the brown glaze for step 5.

3. Dampen the tip of a cotton rag, and remove the grain in small, ribbonlike areas. Work quickly to ensure that the grain marks from the previous step are still wet. The ribbon marks should look clean, with little or no smudging (plate 140). If smudging does occur, wipe the mark clean with a wet cotton swab. Allow the glaze to dry for one or two hours.

4. Use the artists' brush to apply glaze #2 inside the ribbons (plate 141). Then let it dry for one hour.

5. Dip the tapered natural bristle brush into the brown glaze (glaze #1) reserved from step 2. After lightly blotting off any excess glaze onto a rag, gently wisp the remainder over the entire painted surface. Allow the surface to dry completely.

6. Apply the acrylic clear coat over the entire surface.

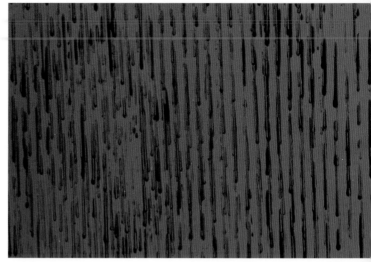

Plate 139

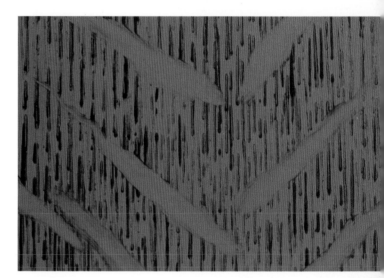

Plate 140

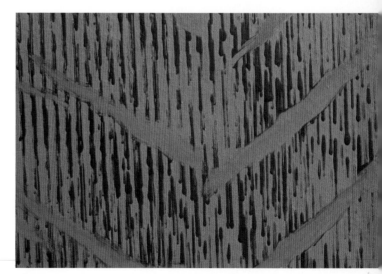

Plate 141

Pattern and Design

*T*HIS CHAPTER INTRODUCES SOME TECHNIQUES THAT USE PAT-
TERN, AND SOME SPECIAL MATERIALS THAT CREATE INTEREST-
ING EFFECTS. THESE FINISHES CAN BE APPLIED TO SURFACES
OF ANY SCALE, BUT MANY OF THEM ARE QUITE LABOR-INTEN-
SIVE. THEY RESULT IN RICH, SUMPTUOUS TEXTURES THAT ARE
WELL SUITED TO FURNITURE AND SMALL AREAS SUCH AS
DOORS, BUT THEY MIGHT BE OVERWHELMING ON A LARGE
SURFACE. COMBINE THESE FINISHES WITH EACH OTHER OR
WITH SIMPLE PAINT TEXTURES TO CREATE INTERESTING PAT-
TERNS, OR USE THEM AS CONTRASTING ELEMENTS TO ENLIVEN
A SMALL ROOM.

Plate 142. The striped walls in this dining room
make the space seem taller, but the pattern is too
subtle to make the room appear cramped. Striping
techniques are described on pages 127–30.

Metallic Paints

Metallic paint contains tiny metal particles that reflect light, and its surface changes appearance depending on the direction and amount of light hitting it. Its appearance is also dependent on the viewer; it shimmers and appears to shift as you move past it. These unique qualities of metallic paint make it an exciting and versatile design option, capable of producing rich textures and subtle designs on projects as small as a music box or as large as a music room.

By nature, metallic paint is fairly translucent; it should be applied over an opaque base color. Use intense colors to highlight the metal and enhance its tone. Silver looks best when applied over blues and greens, gold is best when used on reds and oranges, and copper works well over deep yellow hues.

Water-based metallic paints are hard to find in an ordinary paint store. Art supply stores carry a better selection. If possible, look at the actual paint color before buying the paint (i.e., open the jar or tube; don't trust the color on the lid). Silver paint is generally pretty consistent in color from one brand to the next, but gold paint has a broad color range. It varies from a greenish, brassy tone to a bright yellow. The paints on the yellow end of the spectrum produce a more vibrant finish.

For a durable surface, coat your finished project with a water-based clear finish.

SILVER

Materials

Undiluted, water-based silver metallic paint

Tools

Pencil

Straightedge

Flat synthetic bristle brush

This sample demonstrates the tendency for metallic paint to reveal brush direction. The entire design is created with one color of paint; only the direction of the brush strokes defines the pattern. The horizontal strokes, because of the way the metallic pigment flakes are aligned, generally appear to be brighter than the vertical strokes. The entire pattern changes in appearance too, depending on the light source and the position of the viewer. At times, the pattern fades out entirely, leaving the impression of a solid metal surface. With a change in lighting or point of view, however, the pattern jumps out in sharp contrast.

This pattern is created by first applying a grid to the project surface. Using a straightedge, make faint lines with a pencil. Then fill in each square with silver paint, using the flat synthetic brush to lay down alternating brush strokes (one square horizontal, the next one vertical) to create a simple checkerboard pattern (see plate 144). Once the surface has dried, use a template and pencil to draw a smaller square in the center of each existing painted square (plate145). Repaint each inner square with the silver paint, using the opposite stroke direction from that of surrounding square. This pattern can be rendered loosely, or it can be masked off with tape to achieve crisp, sharp edges.

Plate 143

Plate 144

Plate 145

Metallic Paints

GOLD

Materials

Base coat - Vibrant red enamel

Accent - Water-based gold metallic paint, undiluted

Glaze - 4 parts gold metallic paint and 1 part water

Tools

Pencil

Straightedge

Medium round- or flat-tipped artists' brush

Flat synthetic brush

Clean rags

This sample demonstrates the deep, shimmering quality of metallic paint laid down in layers of varying opacity.

Apply the red base coat using as many coats as necessary to achieve opaque coverage. Since red has poor hiding capacity, two or three coats are necessary for opaque coverage. Afterward, let the project surface dry completely.

Use the straightedge and pencil to apply a light grid for the pattern onto the project surface. Next, using the medium artists' brush, paint a spiral swirl into each square with the undiluted gold paint. Try to make the spirals the same size and shape, but don't worry if they're not all perfect. As long as the initial grid is drawn carefully, the pattern will look consistent (see plate 147). Allow the surface to dry.

Plate 147

Plate 148

Now use a flat synthetic brush to apply the gold glaze to alternating squares in a checkerboard pattern (It's helpful if the brush is the same width as one square). While the glaze is still wet, lightly blot the painted squares with a folded rag to minimize brush marks. Work a few squares at a time so that the glaze doesn't dry before it can be blotted (plate 148). Again, it's all right to be "loose" with your marks; just stay within the grid, and work quickly.

After the previous step has dried, brush the glaze over the entire surface, lightly blotting the wet surface as the glaze is applied. Use the grid lines as borders to establish small working areas; glaze, blot, and move to the next area.

Plate 149. While metallic paint is most commonly used on small objects or as an accent on larger pieces, it can be quite exciting when used on a larger scale. This door, for example, was finished by ragging a gold acrylic paint over a red base color. The gold finish was then incised with the diamond pattern, revealing the red undercoat. Finally, alternating diamonds received another coat of gold paint.

Metallic Paints

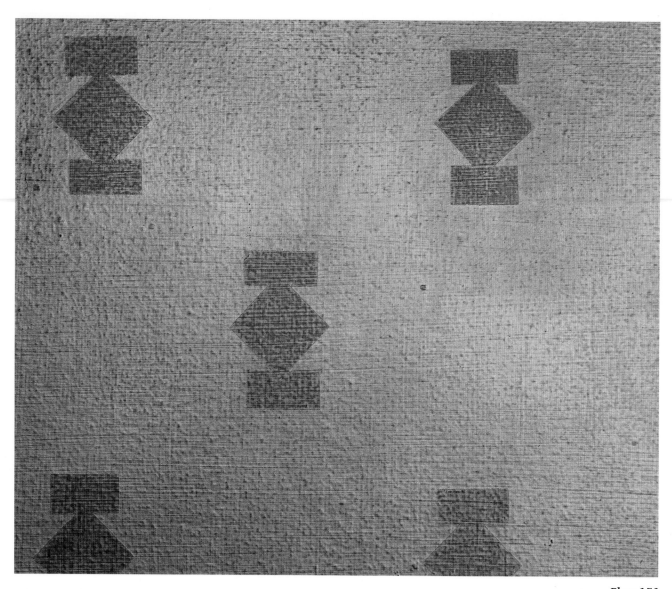

Plate 150

COPPER

Materials

Base coat - Rich yellow low-sheen
   acrylic enamel

Glaze - 4 parts water-based copper paint
   and 1 part water

Tools

Low-tack masking tape

Razor knife

Straightedge

Clean rags

Shallow pan

This example shows the effect of metallic paint applied in a uniform coat, without directional brushwork. The resulting surface is mottled and ambiguous. Because this design contains no grid lines to break the project into easily worked areas, it's difficult to avoid lap marks on surfaces wider than three feet (.9 m). To use this technique on a larger scale, introduce verticals into the design scheme, and lay them out to provide the required breaks.

Apply the base coat to the project surface. For opaque coverage, yellow paint probably requires two to three coats. Then let the surface dry.

The resist pattern in this sample is created using low-tack masking tape. Lay strips of tape onto a fairly porous material such as raw wood, and use a razor knife and straightedge to cut out squares and rectangles. Then press the cut pieces of tape onto the project surface in an evenly spaced pattern (see plate 151).

Now pour the copper glaze into the shallow pan, and use a flat, folded rag to dab it onto the project area. Be sure that the rag is free of wrinkles, and work from one side of the surface to the other (plate 152).

When the surface is dry, peel off the tape to reveal the yellow base coat (plate 153). Apply another coat of copper glaze, blotting it over the entire surface as before.

Plate 151

Plate 152

Plate 153

Crackle Finish

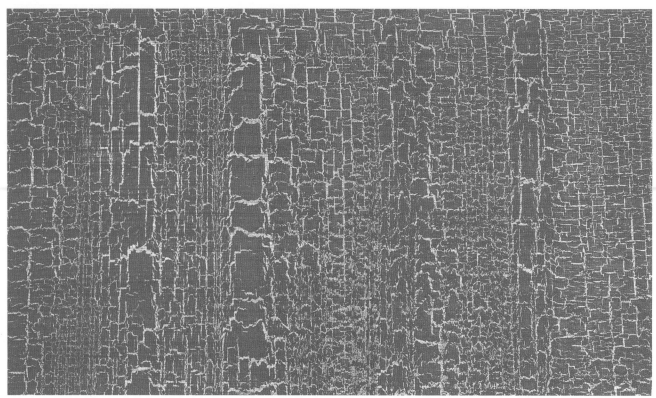

Plate 154

A crackled finish can simulate very old paint, and it's an interesting way to combine colors. To accomplish this finish, apply a film of quick-drying paint over a surface that hasn't completely dried. The resulting trapped moisture forces its way out and cracks the finish. Because this technique relies on tightly controlled drying times, it's limited to small areas. Larger surfaces can be crackled if they are subdivided into areas, such as tiles or panels, no larger than ten square feet (3 square meters).

Materials

Base coat - Whatever color you want to have show through the cracks in the finish (here it is undiluted water-based gold paint)

Glaze #1 - Animal-hide glue thinned with water to a consistency that you can apply with a brush

Glaze #2 - 3 parts low-sheen acrylic enamel and 1 part water

Tools

Synthetic brush

Apply the base color, making sure to obtain opaque coverage, and let the surface dry. When the surface is dry, apply a thin coat of animal-hide glue. The glue should be cut with water until it's just thin enough to brush. Let the glue set up for 15 to 30 minutes or until it is tacky.

When the glue is tacky, use the synthetic brush to apply the finish coat to the project surface. Work swiftly, using even, continuous strokes, and brush all the way across the surface in one stroke. Don't go over your strokes repeatedly; too much brushing in one area can minimize—even negate—the cracking. To ensure consistent results, be sure to practice this technique with some scrap materials prior to the actual application on your project.

Stripes

Stripes are easy patterns to create with water-based paint; the stripes provide convenient borders for work areas, making it possible to avoid overlap marks. Although stripes require a lot of masking, the actual painting is accomplished quickly, and the results justify the careful preparation.

Marking Your Stripes

The first step in creating stripes is to determine their width and number. With a tape measure, determine the length of your wall or other project area in inches (centimeters), and round off the measurement to the nearest inch (centimeter). Then divide the distance by the width that you want for your stripes to determine the total number of stripes. (For example, if the wall is 127 inches, and you want 6-inch stripes, then divide 127 by 6 to get 21.17 stripes.) Round off the result to the nearest whole number, and multiply that number by the width of your stripes (In this example, 21 x 6 = 126). Subtract this result from your actual wall measurement (127 - 126 = 1 inch). Then adjust the last few stripes to account for this discrepancy. (In this example, add 1/8 inch to the final eight stripes on the wall. This will look much better than 21 evenly-spaced stripes with a one-inch stripe at the end of the wall.)

After determining the size of the stripes, mark their locations across the top of the wall with a tape measure (or ruler) and a piece of chalk. (The chalk should contrast with the wall color; use colored chalk if necessary.) Next make a plumb line; tie a small weight such as a metal washer onto one end of a piece of heavy thread or light string. Then tie a knot in the other end—the plumb line should be a few inches (several centimeters) shorter than the height of the wall—and poke a push pin through the knot. When you tack the plumb line to each chalk mark at the top of the wall, the line will hang

Plate 155

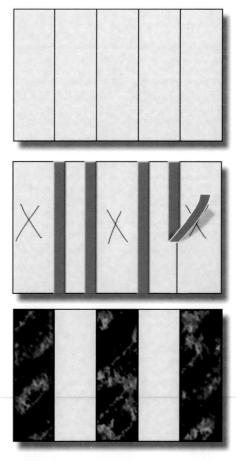

Figure 15

Stripes

plumb, or truly vertical, from the mark. Use the chalk to mark the path of the line—a few light marks between the ceiling and floor should suffice. Repeat the process until you have marked all of the stripes.

Using the chalked marks as guides, mask off the stripes. To make sure that all the stripes will be the same width, mask off alternating stripes, placing the tape on the outside of the marks on every other stripe (see figure 15).

MONOCHROMATIC STRIPES

Materials

Base coat - White low-sheen water-based enamel

Stripes - Flat latex primer or gesso, (or use flat latex as the base coat with enamel stripes)

Glaze - 1 part paint, 1 part water, and 1 part glazing liquid

Tools

Medium-tack masking tape

Synthetic brush

Clean rags

In this example (plate 155), the stripes are created with two different types of paint—flat and enamel—and a glaze that reacts differently to each type of paint.

Apply the base coat, and let it dry. After laying out and masking off the stripes as described above, use a synthetic brush to paint every other one with the latex primer or gesso. Let the surface dry, and remove the tape.

Now use a rag to apply a colored glaze to the entire surface. Working from top to bottom, confine yourself to areas that are about two feet (61 cm) in width, using the edge of a stripe as a stopping point for the work area. (Mask off the edge if necessary.) Notice the difference in appearance of the stripes; the flat stripes absorb the glaze and become darker than the enamel stripes.

Note: This technique can be used on existing walls if they have already been painted with a water-based enamel (eliminate the base coat step). Also, the results don't have to be monochromatic; you can apply the porous primer over a tinted base coat to achieve a different effect.

Plate 156

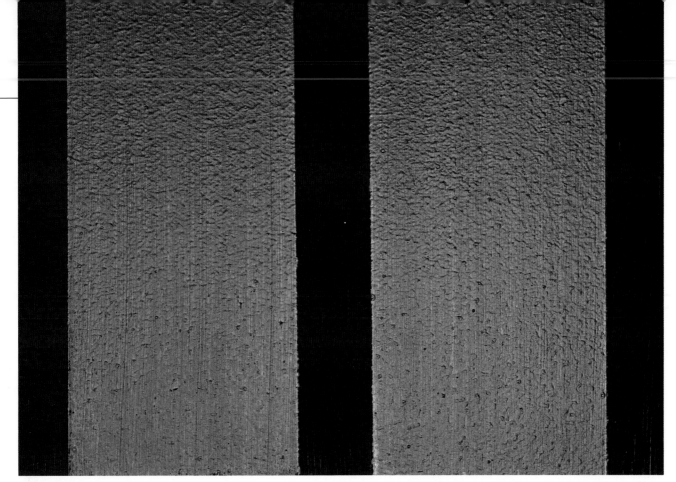

Plate 157

DOUBLE-GLAZED STRIPES

Materials

Base coat - White low-sheen acrylic enamel

Glaze #1 - 1 part paint and 1 part glazing liquid

Glaze #2 - 1 part paint (another color) and 1 part glazing liquid

Tools

Masking tape

Clean rags

Apply the base coat, and allow it to dry. Lay out and mask off the stripes; then use a rag to apply the first glaze to the open stripes. After the surface has dried, remove the tape. Using a rag, apply the second glaze to the entire surface. Remember to work in vertical areas about two feet (61 cm) wide, using the stripes as guides.

For subtle effects, use colors with little contrast (see plate 156).

TAPE STRIPING

Materials

Base coat - Black low-sheen acrylic enamel

Glaze - 1 part charcoal gray, 1 part water, and 1 part glazing liquid

Tools

Low-tack masking tape

Synthetic bristle brush.

Apply the base color, and allow the surface to dry. Using chalk and a plumb line, lay out the stripes, applying the masking tape to the surface. With the synthetic brush, apply the glaze using smooth vertical brush strokes. When the glaze is dry, remove the masking tape to reveal the darker stripes (plate 157).

Stripes

Plate 158

INFORMAL (FREEHAND) STRIPES

Materials

Base coat - Peach-colored low-sheen
 acrylic enamel

Glaze #1 - 1 part orange and 1 part
 glazing liquid

Glaze #2 - 1 part blue and 1 part
 glazing liquid

Tools

Synthetic bristle brush

Clean rags

Apply the base coat, and let it dry. Then use a rag to apply the orange glaze to the entire surface. When the surface has dried, use chalk and a plumb line to lay out the stripes. With the synthetic brush, apply the blue glaze, following the chalk marks to create the stripes (this is easiest if the stripe width and brush width are the same). While the stripes are still wet, blot them with a crumpled rag; this blends them with the texture of the orange glaze. Use the rag to blot some blue glaze lightly over the orange stripes. This final step is essential because it will tone down the contrasting stripes (plate 158).

Sheen Variation

Plate 159

the viewer. The pattern is bold and clear when brightly lit, and it will gradually fade away as the surface recedes into shadow. In order to exploit the full range of contrasts, apply the pattern to a broad, flat surface.

Striped patterns such as the one shown in plate 159 can be achieved by following the instructions on page 129. Be sure to mask each stripe to ensure clean, sharp edges.

To make a repetitive square pattern similar to the one in plate 160, start by applying an opaque base coat to the project surface. Allow the surface to dry for at least one day. Then, with a carpenters' chalk line or a straightedge and a piece of chalk, establish a checkerboard grid (see figure 16), measuring carefully to

These effects are obtained by applying a water-based, clear gloss finish to selected areas of an opaque, low-sheen background. Each pattern is created with low-tack masking tape that is applied to the surface before brushing on the clear finish. This technique is most effective on dark, opaque surfaces; it's not very noticeable on light-colored or textured grounds.

If this method is used to finish a floor, it's recommended that the entire floor be covered with two to three coats of gloss finish, then masked off. Use a final coat of satin finish to create the pattern.

This treatment relies on lighting for its effect. The contrast in sheen ranges from dramatic to subtle depending on the direction and intensity of lighting and on the relative position of

Plate 160

Sheen Variation

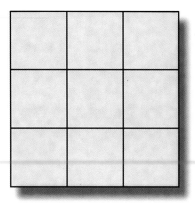

Figure 16

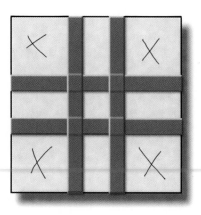

Figure 17

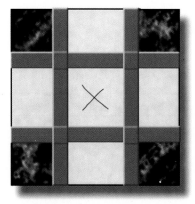

Figure 18

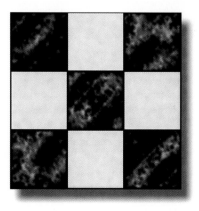

Figure 19

make sure that the squares are uniform in size. Use medium-tack masking tape to mask off the first series of squares (see figure 17); then apply the varnish. After allowing the surface to dry, remove the tape.

If desired, you can continue the process and make a complete checkerboard. Use medium-tack masking tape to mask off the remaining squares (see figure 18), and apply the varnish. When the surface is dry, gently remove the tape (figure 19).

Note: This process can also be used for making a two-colored checkerboard. If you're using contrasting colors, apply the color with the poorest hiding capacity first. For example, for a black and white pattern, apply a white base coat; it's easier for black to cover white than it is for white to cover black.

Block Prints

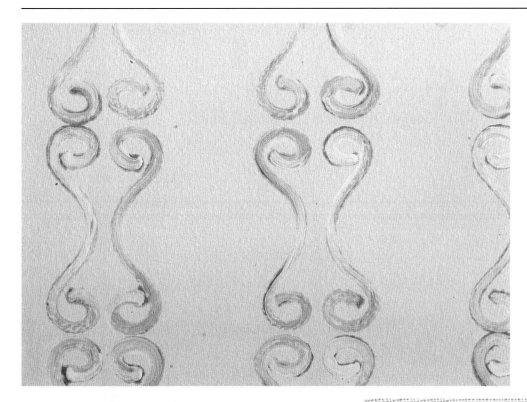

Plate 161

Block printing is an easy and effective way to apply a repetitive pattern to a painted surface. Block prints are created with handmade stamps that have absorbent material such as suede or cotton rope applied to a wooden block.

MAKING PRINT BLOCKS

Determine the size of the printing block after evaluating the project area. Because the design is distributed evenly across the surface of the area, it is possible to imagine the location of the printed designs. Will the pattern be interrupted by doors, windows, or any other breaks in the surface? Since these patterns are created with a solid block, it isn't possible to print a fraction of the image (a stencil can be folded, but a block can't). If possible, size the pattern to avoid interruptions; otherwise, you must create a separate block for each partial image. Another option is to subdivide the project area so that no partial images are required. (Use a contrasting color around the edges of the surface interruptions to frame the printed pattern.)

Plate 162. Top, *rope print block,* bottom, *suede print block*

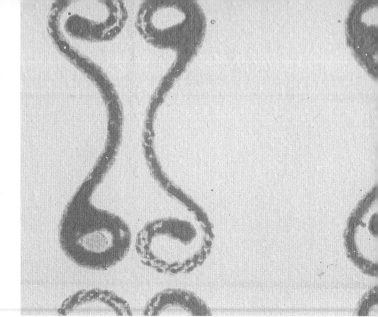

Plate 163

Plate 164

Suede is a good choice for block printing because its finely napped surface holds paint well—resulting in a clear image—and it doesn't shed lint. (Plate 163 shows an image made with a suede print block.) To create a stamp with this material, you must first laminate it until it is thick enough to provide the relief necessary for crisp, clear printing. To laminate suede, first cut it into patches that are roughly the size of the image that you want to reproduce. Spread a thin, even coat of carpenter's wood glue onto the patches, and stack them up until the resulting pad is about 1/4 inch (6 mm) thick; don't spread any glue on the top piece. Weight down the stack with a flat, heavy object such as a pile of books or a board with several bricks placed on top. Let the glue dry several hours; then draw your design onto the suede, and cut it out with a razor knife. Simple shapes without intricate, lacy ornamentation are recommended. Glue the image to an appropriately sized wooden block, and weight it down again until the glue dries.

Cotton clothes line or rope is also an excellent material for block printing, and it's ideal for creating curvilinear designs (see plate 164). To make a printing block with a rope pattern, first draw the intended design onto the wooden block. After winding the rope around the design to determine the exact length required, cut the rope. Glue the ends to prevent them from raveling, but use the glue sparingly, or it will prevent the ends of the rope from absorbing or holding paint. To attach the rope to a wooden block, squeeze a thin, continuous bead of glue onto the block, following the design. Then wind the rope onto the block, and press it onto the glue line. If necessary, attach the ends of the rope with small brads. Put the block—rope side up—onto a stable surface and set a flat, heavy object on top of it until the glue dries.

PRINTING

Materials

Glaze - 1 part low-sheen acrylic enamel, 1 part water, and 1 part glazing liquid

Tools

Straightedge

Chalk

Printing block

Clean rags

Shallow pan

To ensure a uniformly distributed pattern, grid the project surface with chalk and a straightedge. Pour the glaze into the shallow pan sparingly; the depth of the glaze should be less than the depth of the relief on your printing block. Dip the block into the glaze until the relief is loaded. Then lightly dab the excess glaze onto a folded rag. Stamp the images onto the project surface, using the grid lines to register their placement. Allow the surface to dry, and wipe off the chalk lines with a damp rag.

Transfer Paper

chalk lines, and tape down the pattern. Then slip the transfer sheet under the paper, making sure that its coated side faces the project surface. Trace the pattern with a worn pencil or similar dull, pointed object. After the image has been transferred to the entire border, use an artists' brush to fill in the design.

Transfer paper can be used for a variety of tasks. It can be used by itself, following the method described above, to create intricate patterns, or it can be used in conjunction with stencils to add detail to a simpler pattern. Additionally, transfer paper is useful for applying the preliminary designs for mural painting.

Plate 165

Transfer paper is useful for reproducing multiple images whose lines are too delicate to permit the use of a stencil. It's a graphite-coated product that is used, somewhat like carbon paper, to trace an image onto a surface. Transfer paper is sold in sheets and in rolls, and it's available at art supply stores.

To create a pattern using transfer paper, the design must first be drawn onto a sheet of medium-weight paper. Medium-weight paper is your best option because lightweight paper doesn't stand up to repetitive tracing, and heavyweight paper is too thick to transfer the image clearly.

The border pattern shown here is produced by drawing the design motif onto a four-inch-square (10.2-cm) piece of medium-weight paper (see plate 166). Then, using a straight-edge and a piece of chalk, establish two parallel lines four inches (10.2 cm) apart on your project surface. Now subdivide this border into four-inch (10.2-cm) squares. Position your design in the first square on the border, securing it in place with a small piece of low-tack masking tape on the top edge of the paper. Register the edges of the square to your

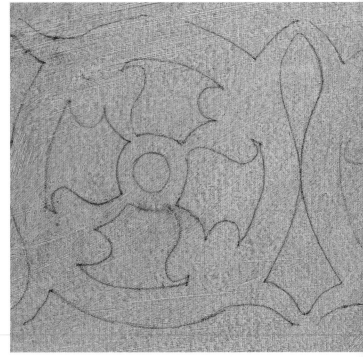

Plate 166

135

Stencils

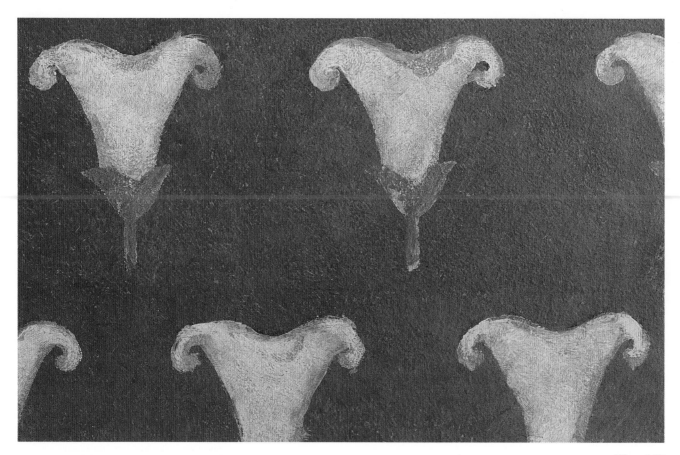

Plate 167

Stenciling is probably the most common way to create a repetitive pattern on a painted surface. Mylar or acetate sheets (which can be purchased at art supply stores) are great for creating stencils. Simply place a sheet over your intended design, and trace it onto the transparent surface with a permanent marker. Then cut out the shape to create the stencil. Heavy paper is a better choice for curvilinear designs because it's easier to cut without tearing. If you use paper, use a transfer sheet to apply the design to the stencil. If you feel reluctant to create your own design, adapt or trace one from a pattern book.

Opaque designs are applied by pouncing small amounts of undiluted paint onto the stencil with a suitable applicator such as a rag, sponge, or stippling brush. Translucent designs

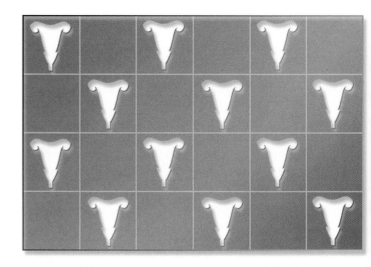

Figure 20

are created by applying glaze in a similar fashion. Be careful when using thin, watery glazes, though; thin glazes can bleed under a stencil, resulting in a poorly defined, runny pattern.

If the surface to be stenciled is a large one, you might save time by creating a stencil sheet with multiple images. It takes a bit longer to create the stencil, but the painting process is much quicker. In addition, be sure to make a single-image stencil to fill in the areas where the stencil sheet doesn't fit.

Before creating the stencil sheet, determine its optimum size by measuring the surface to be stenciled. Use a straightedge and chalk or a carpenters' chalk line to grid off the project area, and cut the stencil sheet to correspond to that grid.

For a simple, alternating pattern, make a stencil sheet with offset rows of images (see figure 20). This allows you to use the corners of the sheet to register the images against the grid, and it also allows you to work from one side of the surface to the other without overlapping wet paint (see figure 21).

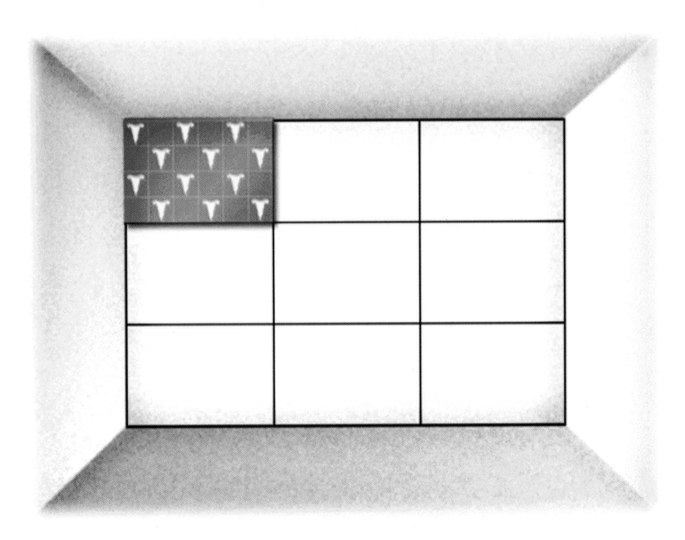

Figure 21

Plate 168

SAMPLE STENCIL

Materials

Base coat - White, low-sheen acrylic enamel

Glaze - 1 part blue, 1 part water, and 1 part glazing liquid

Stencil color - White, low-sheen acrylic enamel

Accent colors - 1 part paint, 1 part water, and 1 part
   glazing liquid

Tools

Stencil

Clean rags

Natural sea sponge

Artists' brush

This sample (plate 167) uses a simple, white, trumpet-shaped floral motif on a blue, rag-finished background. The white paint is sponged undiluted onto the stencil, and the secondary colors are glaze mixtures of yellow and green, which are applied loosely with an artists' brush after the white stenciled pattern has dried.

Another way to add detail to a pattern like this is to use multiple stencils. In this case, create the white, trumpet-shaped base image with the first stencil. After the previous step has dried, apply separate stencils for the leaves and for the yellow core of the flower. Make all stencil sheets the same size, and use the grid to make sure that they relate to each other properly (see figure 21).

NEGATIVE PATTERNING

Materials

Base coat - White, low-sheen acrylic enamel

Glaze #1 - 1 part yellow and 1 part glazing liquid

Glaze #2 - 1 part periwinkle and 1 part glazing liquid

Tools

Stiff cardboard

Construction paper

Razor knife

Spray adhesive

Clean rags

Shallow pan

Stencils

Plate 169

Plate 170

Plate 171

Another method to apply repetitive images is called negative patterning; instead of applying the image to a ground, as is the case with a stencil, the ground is applied around the image. To accomplish this effect, first apply the base coat and let it dry. Next measure the project area to determine the appropriate size of the image, and use chalk to grid the wall accordingly. Create a template made of stiff cardboard cut to the desired shape. Place the template on a stack of construction paper (about ten sheets thick), and use the razor knife to cut around it. When you have cut out enough images, lay them face down on some newspaper, and apply spray adhesive to the backs of the images. Then press them onto the project surface using the grid to place them properly (see plate 169). Be sure to purchase the type of spray adhesive that is used to mount paper temporarily to other surfaces, not the type that bonds your images permanently to the project surface. Following the manufacturer's instructions, spray the adhesive in a well-ventilated area.

Use a rag to apply the first glaze to the entire project surface (plate 170). When the surface is dry, remove the negative stencils (plate 171). Then apply the second glaze to achieve a two-toned pattern.

A variation of this technique calls for undiluted paint to be applied over the negative stencils and makes the use of spray adhesive unnecessary. Cut out the stencils as described above, but use a small loop of tape on the back of each to affix it to the project surface. Using undiluted paint, brush from the center out over each shape. This motion is necessary to prevent the paint from bleeding under the applied shape. Following this technique, paint the entire surface. When the paint is dry, remove the paper images, and use a rag or sponge to apply a glaze over the entire surface. The final step results in a two-toned effect and adds texture to the surface.

Joint Compound Finishes

Joint compound is a slow-drying, plasterlike mud that is used to bridge the seams between individual sheets of drywall, forming a continuous plane. It's available premixed in buckets or boxes at most lumberyards and home-improvement centers, and it comes in several different forms. All-purpose mud is just that—it's used for the initial and finish coats in standard drywall finishing; topping compound is lighter and smoother; and setting-type compound, or "hot mud," is a hard, plasterlike compound that sets in 90 minutes or less. Either all-purpose mud or topping compound is appropriate for this application, but "hot mud" is not recommended.

SKIM COATING WITH JOINT COMPOUND

Materials

Flat latex primer

Joint compound

Tools

Drop cloth

Paint roller and pan

4" (10.2 cm) putty knife

Drywallers' taping knife, at least 10" (25.4 cm) wide

Drywallers' mud pan

"Potato masher" mixing tool

Stiff scrubbing brush

Large sponge

Two 5-gallon (19-l) buckets

Joint compound can be applied in a thin coat to cover the entire project surface. This technique is called "skim coating," and it requires some patience and practice to master. It also requires several specialty tools.

The first of these is a "mud pan"—a rectangular pan, made of sheet metal or plastic, that holds the joint compound. A mud pan has thin, straight edges that are used for cleaning your taping knife.

Drywallers' taping knives are broad, metal spreaders that range from six to 24 inches (15.2 to 61 cm) in width and look like overgrown putty knives. A 10- or 12-inch (25.4- or 30.5-cm) knife is recommended; wider knives are just too unwieldy for a beginner to use.

For this technique, you also need a sanding screen or sandpaper, and a suitable flat holder. Sanding screens are rectangular sheets of cloth mesh that are coated with abrasive particles. The open mesh allows the screen to sand the dried joint compound without getting clogged by the resulting fine dust. These screens are precut to fit onto a pole sander, which is a rectangular, swiveling, foam-backed pad at the end of a four-foot (1.2 m) handle. The handle provides leverage and extended reach. These screens, and some precut sandpapers, also fit onto a hand sander.

Another helpful implement is a mixing tool. This device looks like a two-foot-long (61-cm) potato masher and is useful for thinning the compound with water and for mixing it thoroughly when adding pigments.

Before applying a skim coat to the walls in a room, it's important to cover the floor. Skim coating is a messy process, even for professionals, and although joint compound is water soluble, it sticks tenaciously to everything that it touches, and you can count on having about as much of it on the floor as on the walls. Tape a row of newspaper around the perimeter of the room, and cover the entire floor with drop cloths.

The ideal surface to be skim coated is clean, dry, and flat. If your surface lacks these qualities, clean and prime it to ensure a good bond. (Read more about primers on pages 9–10

To apply the skim coat, first prepare the mud. If the compound you've purchased isn't already in a five gallon bucket, put it into one, add a little bit of water, and use the "potato masher" to mix the water thoroughly into the mud. Add universal pigments at this stage if you're tinting the skim coat. The desired consistency is about the same as that of cream of tomato soup straight from the can. The mix should be slick but not runny. Put the putty knife in the bucket, and keep it covered with the lid or a piece of heavy plastic. Fill the other bucket with clean water and put the scrubbing brush (for

Plate 172

cleaning off the tools) and the sponge (for wiping up messes) into it.

Use the putty knife to scoop the mud into the mud pan until it's about two-thirds full. Hold the pan in your left hand (if you're right-handed) and hold the wide taping knife in your right. When you scoop some mud onto the blade of the knife, load just the front of the blade, and wipe the blade against the inside of the pan to level off the load of mud. Use the sharp edge of the pan to wipe a bit of mud from each end of the blade back into the pan; this prevents the mud from squeezing out past the edges of the knife as you apply it to the walls.

Working from top to bottom, apply the mud in a thin layer to the wall. Hold the knife at a steep angle to the wall, and try to maintain a consistent amount of pressure on the blade as you drag it down the surface. Lay down one band of mud at a time, using long, continuous motions (not short, choppy swipes) to apply it. If necessary, use a clean blade to smooth down the ridges between bands.

Work steadily, and don't try to make the surface look perfect on the first coat; repeated fussing will only frustrate you and make the wall look worse. Smooth down the biggest high

spots while they're wet, and leave the rest for sanding. Don't bother filling voids or hollows while the mud is wet. Instead, fill them with the next coat. If your knife starts to leave long, parallel grooves in the finish, it means that your mud is lumpy and needs to be changed. Scrape out the pan and refill it with fresh mud, and clean the knife with the scrubbing brush.

Continue coating until the entire surface has been skimmed. Then clean your tools thoroughly and immediately with clean water and a scrubbing brush. Allow the surface to dry thoroughly; a thick skim coat might take two days to dry completely. As it hardens, the surface becomes dry to the touch and changes color from gray to white.

When the first coat is dry, use the edge of the taping knife as a scraper to knock down any drips or ridges; then apply a second, lighter coat to the surface. The purpose of the second coat is to fill any inconsistencies in the initial application. When the second coat is dry, lightly sand the entire surface with a medium screen. Use a flashlight or hand-held lamp to apply a raking side-light to the surface, and circle any remaining inconsistencies lightly with a pencil. Apply a light third coat to these areas, and allow them to dry. Finally, sand the entire surface gently with a fine screen, and clean up.

Joint Compound Finishes

ETCHED JOINT COMPOUND

Materials

Base coat - Acrylic primer

Glaze - 1 part low-sheen acrylic enamel, 1 part water, and 1 part glazing liquid

Highlight colors - 1 part paint, 1 part water, and 1 part glazing liquid

Clear acrylic finish

Tools

Transfer paper

Sharp object to use as a stylus (ice pick, screwdriver, letter opener, etc.)

Fine-grit sandpaper

Clean rags

Shallow pan

Fine artists' brush

This technique creates a pattern that actually recedes physically into the painted surface. Start by applying a skim coat to the project surface as described in the preceding section, and be sure to remove the dust from the walls after the final sanding.

When the skim-coated surface is dry and clean, apply a primer coat using a mixture that is four parts acrylic primer and one part water. Allow the surface to dry. This creates a film that is just thick enough to make a nonporous surface. Using transfer paper (as described on page 135), apply a design to your surface (see plate 173). After the design has been applied, use the stylus to incise the pattern into the joint compound (plate 174). Then lightly scuff the etched pattern with the sandpaper to remove loose particles.

Use a rag to apply the glaze to the project surface (plate 175). After it has dried, use an artists' brush to add any accents to the design. Since the pattern itself establishes order on the surface, the accent colors can be applied in a loose, painterly fashion. If you apply the initial glaze heavily to fill in the

etched pattern, the dry joint compound becomes saturated by the glaze, leaving a dark linear pattern. Another option is to apply the glaze lightly. With this method, the glaze doesn't fill the incised design, and white lines result. If the latter treatment is selected, some glaze is bound to seep into the scratches. To touch up a few lines after the glaze has dried, just lightly scratch back into the joint compound with the stylus, and blow out the debris.

Plate 173

Plate 174

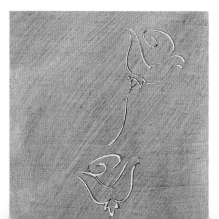

Plate 175

Plate 176

Plate 177

TINTED JOINT COMPOUND

Materials

Flat latex primer

Universal tinting pigments (see below)

Clear acrylic finish

Tools

Drywall tools (mud pan, taping knives, mud mixer, two
   buckets, sponge, scrub brush)

Sanding screen and holder

Floor protection (newspaper, drop cloths, etc.)

If it isn't already clean, dry and flat, clean and prime the
project surface with the flat latex primer; this provides a
surface to which the joint compound will adhere. Allow
the primer to dry.

Tint the mud using universal pigments. Universal tinting pigments are highly concentrated and water-soluble and are
used at paint stores for tinting house paint. They may not be
displayed out on the shelves, but the paint store should sell
them when requested. Using the "potato masher," mix the
pigment thoroughly into the mud. Joint compound tints
quickly, so add the pigment sparingly to achieve the desired
value.

There are several ways to achieve interesting effects with tinted mud. It can be laid in varying depths over a tinted primer
(plate 176), or it can be applied in very thin successive coats,
each tinted a separate color (plate 177). Whatever method is
used, remember to apply a clear coat to the project when
you're finished; it will protect the surface and provide washa-
bility. A clear finish also keeps a "wet" look. As the tinted
mud dries, it becomes pale and chalky; the clear coat restores
depth and intensity to the surface.

Index and Acknowledgments

ACKNOWLEDGMENTS

The authors would like to thank the following people for their support, advice, and technical assistance: Nancy Anderson, Richard Bloomer, Chris Colando, Jim Deitz, Leslie Dierks, Mark Eifert, Bridget Kelsh, Victoria Haven, Chris Miller, Dave Miller, Roberta Miner, Rob Pulleyn, Julie Springer, Gretchen Olson, Jeanne Wasserman, and Robert Yoder. Thanks also to Steve Holladay of Holladay Paint & Wallpaper in Asheville, North Carolina.

INDEX